Better Value Investing

Better
Value Investing

Improve your results as a value investor

Andrew Hunt

Hh

HARRIMAN HOUSE LTD
18 College Street
Petersfield
Hampshire
GU31 4AD
GREAT BRITAIN
Tel: +44 (0)1730 233870
Email: contact@harriman-house.com
Website: www.harriman-house.com

First published in Great Britain in 2015
Copyright © Andrew Hunt

Paperback ISBN: 9780857194749
eBook ISBN: 9780857194978

British Library Cataloguing in Publication Data

A CIP catalogue record for this book can be obtained from the British Library.

 Harriman House

Contents

About the author

Andrew Hunt graduated from Cambridge with a Law degree in 2003. He worked in TV production before moving to Edinburgh in 2006 to join Baillie Gifford, where he works as an Investment Manager.

All views expressed in this book are Andrew's own and not those of Baillie Gifford.

Preface

This book is about value investing in the stock market. Specifically, it explains how to become a better value investor.

True value investors are, and always have been, a rare breed. To the majority of observers, value investors' relentless focus on intrinsic value combined with a peculiarly independent and patient temperament provokes, at best, curious indifference, and at worst, outright contempt. But for a small minority, the value discipline is the most natural and intuitive thing in the world. It just clicks. Warren Buffett has quipped that there must be a value investing gene.

Yet value investors are not all created equal; some are better at it than others. What separates the merely good from the great is the ability to go beyond the proclivity that brought them to value investing in the first place: to improve and to keep progressing. The purpose of this book is to show how value investors can improve in ways that are relatively simple and achievable.

First and foremost, this is a practical book. It has been 15 years in the making, and it draws on personal experience, cutting-edge research, deep thought, wide reading, and thousands of hours of discussion and debate. It is intended for use by personal and professional investors (I am both), and by domestic and global investors alike. The lessons of value investing are universal and can be applied by any investor in any market.

It is also a simple book. In investing, simplicity and practicality go hand-in-hand. The concepts and methods for improvement can be understood and applied by anyone. However, I do assume some basic investing knowledge. To get the most out of the book, you will need to be able to find your way around a set of accounts and understand basic valuation ratios.

The book can be viewed as a coherent framework for value investing, or more likely you will want to take a few of the many ideas and incorporate them into your existing approach. Crucially, these ideas are not just theory or conjecture. I draw heavily on empirical research (which is referenced throughout) and the testimonies of highly successful long-term investors. I am confident you will find many useful and simple ways to improve your investing.

The book is divided into ten chapters. Each chapter identifies and explains a small number of common pitfalls, and offers simple and practical solutions to them, culminating with a short summary and some helpful checklists.

The first two chapters are introductory. Chapter 1 provides a summary of what value investing is and explains its core principles. In Chapter 2, I look at how value investing can go wrong, why it can be improved, and how investors can improve.

Chapters 3, 4 and 5 deal with appraising potential investments. Chapter 3 explains the importance of properly assessing financial strength when choosing value shares, and goes through the techniques that should be used to thoroughly appraise a company's financial position. Chapter 4 outlines how to assess management and to complete due diligence checks, and includes a handy list of factors to consider when doing so. In Chapter 5 I look at valuation – specifically, how and when to use a range of different valuation techniques to achieve better results.

The remaining chapters focus on investment strategy. Chapters 6 and 7 deal with when and where to look for investments. Chapter 6 is an in-depth exploration of contrarian investing and how it relates to value investing, including how to invest during crises. Chapter 7 examines how global and small-cap approaches to investing can enhance returns.

Chapter 8 explains how to construct and maintain a portfolio of value shares. A key component of portfolio construction is ensuring sufficient diversification, so that the portfolio is not overwhelmed by unexpected events. The chapter then outlines how to buy and sell shares in a more disciplined and effective manner. This process of portfolio rebalancing is a vital but often neglected element of successful value investing.

Then we come to Chapter 9, which in my opinion is the most important and the most rewarding. I begin by describing how investors invariably do not achieve the results they expect in large part because they fail to stick to the strategy they set out to follow.

While all investors struggle to stick to their plans, value investors are especially prone to this because of behavioural pitfalls and social pressures. I detail some powerful methods to overcome these pitfalls and execute a value investing strategy consistently. This includes an examination of *checklists* – an innovation that is gaining increasing attention in many fields, both within finance and beyond.

Lastly, Chapter 10 considers the importance of ongoing improvement and lifelong learning, before concluding with a summary of the key messages covered throughout.

When value investing is conducted well, there is an innate pleasure about it that transcends the mere end of making money. I hope that in reading this book, you will discover ideas that are sufficiently valuable to carry with you throughout your investing life, and that bring you a little more of that pleasure.

Andrew Hunt

Edinburgh, Spring 2015

PART I.
Introduction

CHAPTER 1

Value Investing 101

1.1 What is value investing?

"Value investing is buying securities at a significant discount to their underlying value and holding them until their value is realized. The element of the bargain is the key to the process."

Seth Klarman[1]

I N THIS CHAPTER I'LL GO THROUGH THE BASICS OF value investing.

Value investing is defined by a set of principles rather than hard and fast rules. These principles were popularised and articulated by Benjamin

---

1. Klarman, S. A., *Margin of Safety: Risk-Averse Value Investing Strategies for the Thoughtful Investor* (New York: Harper Business, 1991).

Graham nearly a century ago in two famous books, *Security Analysis* and *The Intelligent Investor*.

The practice of trading shares in businesses goes back centuries. Historically, shares were seen as highly speculative investments: a tool for punters to take bets on the short-term moves in a company's or an economy's fortunes. This view can be well understood, as early share trading proved tumultuous on more than one occasion, such as during the infamous Mississippi and South Sea bubbles. Conservative investors meanwhile bought bonds, with steady and predictable cash flow profiles.

In the early twentieth century, a number of people – notably Benjamin Graham and John Burr Williams – began to demonstrate shares could be more than just a tool for speculation. Shares, after all, represent ownership of underlying businesses. And businesses have an *intrinsic value*, which can be found by discounting the cash they make for shareholders over their lifetimes.

So if an investor can estimate the value of the underlying business, and divide it by the number of shares, he can find the true value of the shares. Once the value of the share has been estimated, all the investor needs to do is buy shares trading at a big discount to their intrinsic worth, and turn a profit by waiting for their prices to converge with his assessed value. In practice this can happen in a number of ways. For example: the share price may rise as other investors realise the share is undervalued, the investor may receive his value through ongoing dividends, or the company or its assets may get bought.

This is the core of value investing: take a share, work out the value of the underlying business it represents, then buy the share when it's priced well below that level and sell it when it's priced above that level. Warren Buffett, the most successful investor of all time, famously described this process as, "Buying a dollar for forty cents."

1.2 Why choose value investing?

There are two reasons investors choose to become value investors. The first is that it *should* work and the second is that it *does* work.

Value investing should work because it is supported by a logical framework. A share represents ownership of an underlying company. It has no other practical value or purpose – you cannot eat a share, live in a share, or enjoy it as a work of art. A share's value derives solely from the value the underlying business creates for its shareholders.

Other techniques for buying and selling shares exist and sometimes enjoy periods when they seem to work very well, but they tend to go awry because ultimately they are not anchored to the reality of the situation. For example, take momentum investing. A momentum investor buys shares because the share price has gone up, but ultimately the share price must depend on the value of the underlying business. So if it goes wrong and the share price moves against him, the momentum investor has nothing to fall back on. In the same situation, where the price moves against a value investor, he can be reassured by his knowledge of the business' underlying value.

Theory is one thing, but does it work in practice?

The answer is a resounding yes. Over the long run, investors following a value-based approach have beaten the field by a very wide margin. Perhaps the most famous is Warren Buffett, whose record and wealth stands as testimony to the success of his approach. But Buffett is by no means the only one. In a now famous speech, entitled 'The Superinvestors of Graham-and-Doddsville',[2] Buffett went through the astounding records of a group of fellow investors, all of whom were following value-based approaches.

In recent decades, improvements in IT and statistical analysis have enabled experts to back-test value approaches. These studies typically involve testing a strategy of buying a basket of the cheapest shares as defined by measures such as low price-to-book (P/B), low price-to-earnings (P/E), low price-to-sales (P/S) or high dividend yield, and

---

2. Buffett, W. E., 'The Superinvestors of Graham-and-Doddsville', *Hermes: The Columbia Business School Magazine* (Fall 1984), pp.4-15.

measuring the performance compared to the market over a number of years or decades.

Thousands of such studies have been done over time periods ranging from a few months to 70 or 80 years, and covering markets all over the world. What is striking about them is how consistent the results have been. Barring a few exceptional periods (typically around speculative bubbles), a strategy of buying the cheapest shares has worked everywhere, from the raciest emerging markets to economic laggards like Japan. And it has worked through booms and recessions, decade after decade.

Perhaps more incredibly, this simple approach that almost anyone can learn has continued to win, even as financial markets have become more sophisticated. Individual value investors adhering to the basic principles are still getting the better of PhDs and highly-paid bankers with access to enormous resources.

So what are these magic principles?

1.3 The fundamentals of value investing

Principle 1: It all starts with intrinsic value

When considering whether to buy or sell a share, the value investor has one overriding question: *what's it worth?*

In order to answer that, he must make an assessment of the company's *intrinsic value* (otherwise referred to as absolute value). The intrinsic value is what the company would be worth to a level-headed, private buyer who intends to hold the company over the remainder of its lifetime.

In order to work out an intrinsic value, the investor needs to consider many aspects of the company – its competitive position, growth prospects, management, balance sheet strength and so on – and bring these factors together into an assessment of intrinsic value.

Ben Graham defined this process of selecting companies based on their underlying worth as *investing*. Everything else he defined as speculation. Speculating is neither immoral nor illegal, and it may even work now and again. It is just that value investors like Graham found value investing more financially rewarding.

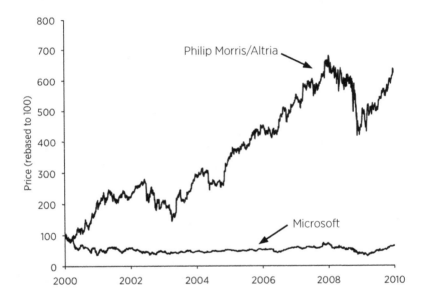

Chart 1.1. Philip Morris/Altria and Microsoft, 2000-2010

In practice great companies can be overvalued (and therefore make terrible investments), while lesser companies can be undervalued (and therefore make great investments). For example, back in 2000, Microsoft looked like a great company. It had a very strong market position thanks to Windows, a visionary owner and exciting growth prospects, thanks to the internet and tech booms that were underway. By contrast, cigarette-maker Philip Morris (now called Altria) looked an awful place to put your money. Its customer base was shrinking, with governments piling increasing pressure on tobacco companies. Moreover, it faced billion dollar law suits and a PR disaster from the millions of victims of smoking.

Over the subsequent ten years, Microsoft delivered a total return of -36%, while Philip Morris/Altria returned 506%! This is shown in Chart 1.1. Curiously, many of the successful value investors who bought Altria around 2000 were buying Microsoft a decade later in 2010. How things change! It is a perfect illustration of how value investing is determined by the price versus the value, rather than by the company itself.

The point is that everything has its price. What makes a share a good candidate for a value investor is not that it is a great company (although it may be), but that it is greatly undervalued.

Principle 2: The margin of safety

Having come up with an intrinsic value, value investors then apply a large discount (usually a third or more) when setting the price they are willing to pay for a share. For example, if you were to value a share at 75 pence, then, after applying a margin of safety of one-third, the maximum price you would be willing to pay for this share would be 50 pence. This is the *margin of safety*.

While most investors will typically use a margin of safety of a third to a half, the exact amount can vary. For example, you may want a larger margin of safety where uncertainty is especially high (such that you have low confidence in the assumptions underpinning your valuation) or where you are finding far more opportunities than you can invest in. However one-third should always be regarded as the minimum to ensure there is a worthwhile gain and to counter potential over-optimism in your valuations.

The margin of safety serves two purposes. The first is to achieve superior investment returns. If you buy a company for around its intrinsic value, you can expect only a market-like rate of return on the investment. However, if you only buy companies that are selling at much less than their intrinsic value, you should be able to get a much higher rate of return.

The second reason is to provide extra protection against being wrong. When you are assessing the value of a company, there is a lot of guesswork and uncertainty involved, so it is easy to go wrong. As a result, it is worth adding an extra buffer in.

The following table illustrates neatly how the extra margin of safety provides protection and enhances returns.

	Things go badly	Things go okay	Things go very well
Pay a normal price	Lose a lot	Neutral	Make a little
Pay no more than conservative value	Lose a little	Make a little	Make a lot
Pay no more than conservative value + margin of safety	Neutral	Make a lot	Make a fortune!

Table 1.1. How an extra margin of safety provides protection and enhances returns

This is no different from, say, catching a plane. You never know exactly how long it is going to take to get to the airport and through check-in as there can always be hiccups, so most travellers leave themselves a little more time than they expect they'll need.

Moreover, human psychology provides a further rationale for the margin of safety. Many recent behavioural studies have found that people all over the world tend to be over-optimistic most of the time, about everything from how much they expect to earn to how long they think they'll live. Over-optimism is a vital trait for survival: it pushes us to take risks and try new things, it keeps us happy and hopeful rather than suicidal, and drives us to keep working rather than giving up. Indeed, studies have also found that highly successful people tend to be especially prone to over-optimism.

Unfortunately, investing is one of the places where over-optimism can be dangerous. Over-optimism causes investors to disregard the risks and overvalue the opportunities, causing them to lose money. A healthy margin of safety serves as a valuable defence against this.

The final point on margin of safety is that it can be applied in a much more holistic sense than just valuation. For example, investors may demand a margin of safety in terms of financial strength, thereby avoiding financially weak companies that cannot survive if things go worse than expected. In a portfolio context, investors also talk about having a margin of safety in terms of their risk management. This means being sufficiently diversified and avoiding using too much leverage to ensure that the portfolio is not wiped out if a number of investments perform worse than expected. These perspectives are considered more fully later.

Principle 3: Mr Market

Share prices can fluctuate wildly in either direction in a very short space of time. While good and bad news may come and go day by day, often this news and the radical gyrations of the market in response to it have little effect on the long-term, underlying value of a company's shares.

What is happening is that investors are driven by their speculative instincts, becoming overly emotional about short-term events, or even about price movements themselves. A few bits of good news and a decent economic outlook and they become over-exuberant, willing to pay sky-high valuations. But a string of disappointments or a weak economy, and they become overly pessimistic, when almost no price is too low.

This is what we call overreaction. Overreaction is what creates investing opportunities, but only for investors who can keep their heads. This requires sticking to a longer-term view, anchored squarely to the fundamentals of the business. An investor must accept that good and bad periods will come and go, and that these should be adjusted for in a sober manner.

To illustrate the point, Ben Graham came up with the concept of *Mr Market*. Imagine Mr Market is your business partner and he has a habit of offering to sell you his stake in the business every day. He doesn't mind if you ignore him or take him up on the offer. He also has one other peculiar feature: Mr Market suffers from a sort of bipolar disorder, swinging wildly between great optimism and great pessimism.

So some days when the business is going well, Mr Market comes in cock-a-hoop, waxing lyrical about how he owns the best company in the world and offering to sell it to you for a crazily high price. On other days when trading is more difficult, Mr Market gets very depressed; he now believes it is an awful business that is sure to go bust imminently, and he is practically offering to give you his stake.

The temptation is to pay attention to Mr Market's *behaviour*. After all, he is dramatic, entertaining, persuasive and compelling. And yet, if you do get caught up in Mr Market's behaviour and opinions, you will end up buying his shares at a very high price and missing out when he's offering them very cheaply.

This happens to real shares all the time as markets swing between extremes of optimism and pessimism. Rising shares give the illusion of success and high returns, encouraging investors to pile in deeper and deeper. Conversely, falling shares reinforce negative attitudes, driving prices down further. In fact, when share prices fall, the shares are usually getting further and further away from the underlying worth to which they must eventually revert. It is easy to allow all this action to influence your judgment. Most likely it will lead you to buy (or refrain from selling) rising shares, and to sell (or refrain from buying) falling shares.

Instead, the successful value investor must *focus on Mr Market's price, not his behaviour*. This means buying shares when their prices are knocked right down and uncertainty and pessimism are rife, then selling them when they're sky-high and everyone feels sure of their glittering prospects. It is often said that you should buy shares like groceries, loading up when they're cheap and shunning them when dear. As famous value investor Chris Browne put it, "I always try to buy shares when they're on sale, no matter where the sale is."

It all sounds rather straightforward. Unfortunately, buying low, selling high and getting the better of Mr Market is remarkably difficult in practice. As we'll see later on, the great hurdle to value investing is temperament. It sounds so easy and yet it is strangely difficult to do in practice. Even the most successful value investors find it really tough.

Principle 4: The need for patience

What makes Mr Market such a source of opportunity is that you are always free to ignore him or to take him up. The stock market is even better; every day you are offered instant prices on thousands of businesses and you are completely free to buy or sell any of them or to do nothing.

In few areas of life do you get so many choices along with the freedom to take them up exactly when you want. Warren Buffett compares it to a baseball game in which the hitter has an infinite number of pitches. He doesn't have to swing at any of them. In such a situation, the hitter should be willing to let hundreds or thousands of pitches just pass him by, and wait for the perfect 'fat pitch' – just the right height, right pace, line and length – at which point he should swing for the fences. If such a game were to exist, the hitter should hit perfect home runs every time. All he needs is the discipline of patience.

In practice, finding great bargains is quite rare. Most of the time value investors are not trading. Instead, the time is spent considering lots of companies and how much they're worth, then passing them over for the time being, until they are sufficiently cheap. Often this will mean stalking businesses for years, keeping an eye on the price and anything major that might affect the intrinsic value, ready for when the perfect moment comes.

Having found a bargain and bought in, there still isn't much to do, other than keeping an eye out for any major events, governance matters and where the price is. Most of the work is already done. So long as the business is financially sound and was purchased below its value, what more is there to do? It only gets interesting if it gets a lot cheaper, when it is time to buy more, or very fashionable and expensive, when it is time to sell.

Charley Ellis described this attitude as "benign neglect." People are often surprised by reputable investors running billions, who seem to be virtually inert. Investing really is just waiting for the right opportunity, then waiting some more for the value gap to close. It is not listening and reacting to Mr Market. Ellis could not have put it better when he said, "In investing patience and fortitude – or benign neglect – are more beneficial than activity. To rephrase the familiar admonition: 'Don't just do something, stand there!' "[3]

Principle 5: Simplicity is more important than precision

As any attempt at valuation involves making predictions of the future, it is inherently uncertain. In recent years there has been a trend towards ever more complicated valuation models, as analysts have enjoyed access to more detailed information and increasingly powerful computers.

However, all this detail and complexity rarely results in more accurate predictions, and often leads investors to go seriously awry. Many of the most extreme valuations at the height of the tech bubble were underpinned by exceptionally complex models dreamt up by investment bankers. Some ran to hundreds of pages and were packed with complicated mathematics, yet they still turned out to be absolutely wrong.

It is far better to accept that valuation can never be an exact science. Instead, strive to be roughly right rather than precisely wrong. It is always worth remembering Aswath Damodaran's suggestion, "When valuing an asset use the simplest model that you can."

Principle 6: The need for flexible and diverse approaches to valuation

Not all valuation techniques are applicable, or indeed possible, for the many different situations you are likely to come across. For example, a high quality growing franchise would probably require a discounted cash flow model to take account of its earnings power and growth prospects.

---

3. Ellis, C. D., *Winning the Loser's Game: Timeless Strategies for Successful Investing* (New York: McGraw-Hill Professional, 2002).

On the other hand, a company in a rapidly failing industry may need to be valued based on the liquidation value of its assets. Taking another example, a biotech firm may need a scenario analysis to reflect the binary outcomes from its potential treatments.

As well as absolute valuation, there are also relative value measures. This is where you compare a company's valuation metrics to its peer group, the whole stock market or to its history. While relative valuation is a useful sense-check, it is generally not enough on its own.

Often it is sensible to try more than one valuation method on the same share. This serves as a useful sanity check and to highlight key elements in your assumptions. As ever, the aim of all this is to come up with a conservative estimate of intrinsic value, such that, when combined with a substantial margin of safety, you can feel very confident that you are getting an excellent deal.

It is not the purpose of this book to go into detail on valuation methods – there are many good books available that do so. Three particularly good resources on valuation are: *Security Analysis* by Benjamin Graham and David Dodd; *Value Investing: From Graham to Buffett and Beyond* by Bruce Greenwald, Judd Kahn, Paul Sonkin and Michael van Biema; and *The Little Book of Valuation* by Aswath Damodaran.

Table 1.2 provides a summary of some of the more popular techniques.

Method	What it is	When to use it
Discounted cash flow (DCF)	A DCF valuation adds up all future predicted free cash flows and discounts them to their present values. The big risk (as with all valuation techniques), is that it relies on some key assumptions and changing any of them can yield vastly varying results.	When you have a good idea about the future cash flows for at least several years into the future.

Method	What it is	When to use it
Shareholder payout discount model	Valuing a share based on its shareholder distributions (i.e. dividends + buybacks) and discounting them back to present value, such that: value = shareholder distributions per share / (discount rate - growth rate of distributions)	When you have a good feel for what future shareholder distributions, returns and growth are likely to be.
Reproduction value	An estimate of what it would cost to recreate the business from scratch. This involves estimating the replacement costs of the tangible assets, as well as intangible values, such as R&D costs, and sales and marketing costs. If companies are trading well below reproduction value, new capacity is unlikely to come in and existing capacity will decline, thereby raising earnings and value. But if companies are trading above reproduction value, new capacity will come in, dragging down returns and valuations to reproduction cost.	Where the business is viable but has no clear competitive advantage, reproduction cost is an appropriate valuation measure.
Liquidation value	An estimate of what the business would be worth if it were simply shut down, all of its assets were sold and all its liabilities were paid off. This is found by working through the accounts and generally discounting the assets. Often a 'net-net' valuation is used as a proxy for liquidation value. Where: net-net = 2/3 x (current assets - total liabilities including prefs and minority interests)	If a company is in decline or in serious trouble, this is one of the most conservative ways to value it.

Method	What it is	When to use it
Earnings power value	A simple valuation technique based on a normalised adjusted earnings measure and assuming no future growth.	Where little or no growth is expected or where you want to use future growth as the margin of safety.
Appropriate multiple	If you have an idea of what certain metrics (such as normalised profitability) are for a business, you can back out those assumptions into an appropriate multiple of sales, book value or earnings. For example: price/book ratio = (normalised return on equity x payout ratio) / (cost of equity - growth rate)	When you have a feel about what the normalised inputs should be. Most of the time price/book and enterprise value/sales are more useful than earnings or cash flow multiples, as book values and sales tend to be more stable.
Scenario analysis	Ascribing probabilities and valuations to more than one different scenario. For example, a biotech company may be worth $1bn if its drug gets commercialised and $0 if not. Ascribing a 30%-70% probability would give a value of (0.3*$1bn) + (0.7*$0bn) = $0.3bn.	When different potential outcomes will lead to very different valuations.
Relative valuation	Comparing multiples with peers, the market and the company's long-run history.	As a sense-check.

Table 1.2. Summary of the popular valuation techniques

Principle 7: Value and growth are joined at the hip... but not all growth is valuable

For many investments, future growth is a key component in assessing value. While the prospects of rapid growth can seem very appealing, often it turns out to be worthless. There are three difficulties with valuing growth.

Firstly, growth is only valuable where it is within a franchise. That is, the growing company has a unique competitive position that prevents others taking advantage of the opportunity. If the company has no special advantage (and most do not), it will have to compete evenly with others for those growth opportunities, so the overall long-run return on any investment is only likely to be at market-like rates or even lower. This is because the best return a company with no franchise can hope for when reinvesting its money in growth opportunities is a market-like return. This is likely to be no better than if it returned the money to shareholders and they then reinvested it in the wider market.

Secondly, even where growth is valuable, it may not be sustainable for very long. A lucrative and growing business will quickly attract aggressive competitors and imitators keen to muscle in. Eventually, the growth acts like an anchor, as demand is satiated and diseconomies of scale start to kick in.

Finally, growth – like everything else in the future – is highly uncertain. It may seem very likely and yet it may never happen.

Because of these three difficulties, value investors tend to be very cautious when valuing future growth prospects. Different investors tackle this in different ways. Some try to be conservative in their future assumptions, and many go further, refusing to pay at all for future growth and treating it instead as the margin of safety.

1.4 Summary

- At the heart of value investing is working out an intrinsic value for the underlying business. This is where you bring together all you know about the company into an estimate of its true worth.

- This can be tricky, so try and think long term and use a range of simple techniques (such as those outlined in the previous table) to check your assumptions.

- Be independent in your assumptions. Use your own information and insights, not Mr Market's.

- Remember, a company is a good investment because it is grossly undervalued. Great companies can be bad investments, while troubled companies can often be great investments.

- Be conservative and always use a healthy margin of safety. The more conservative you are, the more upside there will be in the investments you choose.

- Be patient. It can take a long time to find a great bargain and even longer for it to work out.

- Value investing is logical, practical and successful. However, sticking to the core underlying principles is remarkably difficult.

CHAPTER 2.

Improving the Approach

2.1 Even value investing can go wrong

Every day we benefit from the long history of human progress. Since the dawn of time, people have sought to better their lives and the lives of others. Just look around you – everything from cars to holidays to washing powder is constantly being improved and updated, as people strive for better.

So the question is: why should investing be any different? Why should investors be cut off from the rapid rate of progress seen in other spheres of society?

When Ben Graham constructed his brilliant theory of value investing almost a century ago, the world was a very different place. In the decades since, investors have benefitted from enormous technological advances, the ability to back-test investment approaches, the records and experiences of *super-investors*, behavioural finance theory, greater access to information and computing power, and the rise of international investing and emerging markets. Today we know far more and we have far more choices. *Surely investors can do better now than in Graham's time?*

And yet, the opposite has happened. Along with much of the financial services industry, many value investors lost their way. Since 2008, illustrious records have been desecrated by years of poor performance. For example, the US Investor Bill Miller whose high profile Legg Mason Value Trust beat the S&P 500 for a record 15 consecutive years between 1991 and 2005, saw his fund subsequently underperform by nearly 10% p.a. over the next six years, before he finally stepped down. Worse still, many of those who claimed to be value investors (particularly in the private equity sphere) used vast amounts of leverage, exacerbating their problems, in some cases to the point of bankruptcy. This wasn't supposed to happen. Value investors had long been seen as the traditional saviours of bear markets, ready to step into the financial storm and pick up the bargains. But this time they were the victims.

What went wrong?

The first problem was simple hubris. Investors following any sort of cheap value strategy enjoyed a fantastic run after the tech bubble burst. The trouble with value investing in the period from 2001 to 2008 was you could make a lot of mistakes and still make a lot of money! It all seemed so easy; everyone claimed to be running some sort of value strategy, and while the money rolled in these investors didn't bother to look out for risks or ways to improve. Value investors became arrogant. Value investing became a victim of its own success.

A related problem – and something that has happened many times to value investors – is that it is easy to become blinded by simple cheapness. There is a deeply visceral appeal to the idea of buying something cheap. Just look at how shoppers are drawn to sales or special offers. The sheer power of this instinct can leave you blinkered. Most of the time, cheap companies are cheap for a reason.

As we'll see later on, one of the most underappreciated facts about value investing is that most cheap (low multiple) shares actually *underperform*. Most of the time, just buying cheap isn't enough; if you simply purchase any old cheap shares as a broad approach, you are likely to be disappointed. Instead, value investors have to go beyond the primitive allure of a low multiple.

Separating the sheep from the goats

Developing a more successful value strategy requires an understanding of what can go wrong with value investing as well as what can go right. I've spent my career at one of the world's most reputable and successful *growth* investing firms (yes, long-term growth investing really can work too). Instead of hanging out with the value club, I went and hooked up with their ideological opposites.

Thanks to this more critical perspective, I have been able to identify the biggest problems most value investors encounter and to find ways to overcome them. In doing so, I have drawn not just on theory, but on empirical research, the testimonies of successful investors and extensive personal experience.

What is most striking about all this research is that it keeps pointing to the same things. When value investors make mistakes, it's nearly always down to the same handful of fairly simple reasons. Understanding those risks and developing ways to avoid them is what this book is all about.

2.2 Surviving and prospering

Investing is no different from any other activity. If you want to improve, you have to be willing to really work at it. And like other activities, at the start, improving is easy. The simple act of just doing something over and over again will lead to better results. But soon, simply *doing* is not enough. This is where most people plateau. Think about amateur golfers: when they start, they improve very quickly thanks to the training and learning. Then they quickly reach a point where they stop improving and their handicap stays the same.

So how do you keep getting better? Across a wide variety of fields, from music to sports, it has been found that those who succeed at the highest level don't just work hard, but work in a very specific and unusual way. Firstly, they are incredibly self-critical; they constantly look for weaknesses and seek feedback on where they need to improve. And having got that feedback, they focus their efforts on fixing those very things that they're weakest at.[4]

In investing, this means spending a lot of time carefully going over mistakes, trying to uncover potential risks and working especially hard at fixing flaws in your approach. Unfortunately, this involves taking hard criticism (from others as well as yourself) and devoting most effort to the elements of investing you find most difficult.

This is very hard to do. We would all prefer just to keep doing what we're already good at and find easy, and none of us likes looking back at our mistakes or receiving criticism. Yet this is the course that offers us the surest way to major improvement.

Deliberate and mindful

A tough, self-aware approach does not just apply to individuals: it is even more important for investment organisations and teams. Karl Weick is an organisational expert who has spent his career examining how organisations react in times of rapid change, when they come under the most pressure.[5] Under these circumstances, many seemingly successful groups unravel rapidly, while others are able to adapt and thrive.

Weick calls these latter groups High Reliability Organisations, or HROs. Many HROs operate in areas where they face extreme pressure, rapidly evolving situations and the potential for disaster on an ongoing basis; yet they very rarely fail. Examples include nuclear reactors, aircraft carriers and A&E departments.

What makes HROs so good at dealing with change? Weick identifies their key attribute as "collective mindfulness." Mindful organisations are incredibly self-aware. They communicate openly and regardless of

---

4. Ericsson, K. A., Krampe, R. Th. and Tesch-Römer, C., 'The Role of Deliberate Practice in the Acquisition of Expert Performance', *Psychological Review* 100:3 (1993), pp.363-406.
5. Weick, K. E. and Sutcliffe, K. M., *Managing the Unexpected: Resilient Performance in an Age of Uncertainty* (New York: John Wiley & Sons, 2007).

seniority. They encourage dissent and criticism to the point of actually rewarding members for speaking out, admitting mistakes or identifying potential problems. They are constantly on the lookout for even the smallest mistakes or near misses. When they spot one, they go over it carefully, not in order to find blame but to prevent a repeat.

Taking a mindful approach is what will lead you beyond the visceral appeal of just buying cheap. Learning and experience allows the approach to be honed in a way that eradicates the most costly errors. In doing so, your investment process will become increasingly defined by what needs to be avoided. It should be increasingly deliberate. As Weick observes, "Every strategy can be restated as mistakes that must be avoided, threats to sidestep and bullets to dodge... to be more deliberate means to be more thorough in articulating mistakes you don't want to make."[6]

In the process of becoming more deliberate, you will also become more discerning. As legendary value investor Chris Browne wrote, "My best friend when it comes to building my inventory of value investing opportunities is the no-thank-you-pile."[7] Ideas are not generally hard to find, especially nowadays with screens and endless ideas from brokers, the internet and the media. Successful investing is at least as much to do with deciding what to pass up on as what to actually buy.

Today's investors face a rapidly changing and extremely volatile landscape in which success rates are brutally low. Developing the right mindset is not only necessary to help you improve, but to avoid the cataclysmic disasters that periodically wipe out so many.

---

6. *Ibid.*
7. Browne, C. H. and Lowenstein, R., *The Little Book of Value Investing* (New York: John Wiley & Sons, 2006).

2.3 The three dimensions of investment strategy

When constructing your value strategy, or indeed any strategy, it is helpful to think in terms of three essential pieces. As you read this book, having these three perspectives and appreciating where each element fits in will help you organise and define your approach most clearly.

1. **Set out your investment approach** – i.e. work out what you want to do. This is the most obvious element. In practice, I think most investors fail because they do not get beyond this first part.

2. **Define what you need to avoid** – No matter what the approach is, it will open up the investor to certain types of error. An enormous edge can be gained if you can identify those errors and develop your framework so as to avoid them. This is non-intuitive and takes time.

3. **Be able to execute your approach** – It is easy to underestimate how incredibly difficult it is to actually follow even a simple plan. In practice there are enormous psychological, financial and practical barriers, all of which militate against achieving even the most simple of investment strategies.

PART II.

Company Analysis

CHAPTER 3.

Financial Strength

3.1 Introduction

Understanding financial strength and appreciating its importance is perhaps the most vital lesson for value investors. While assessing financial strength can be a complex and often difficult task, it is a sure-fire way to improve investment results over time.

Assessing financial strength requires a multi-faceted approach. This is especially important to emphasise at the start. Too many investors think that financial strength is just about the amount of debt on the balance sheet, or that it can be assessed by looking at a single metric.

Unfortunately, things are not that simple. There are many potential problem liabilities other than debt, some of which may not even be on the balance sheet. And a lot of the time, the company's near-term liabilities and cash flows are at least as important as the long-term liabilities.

Many investors learn this the hard way, buying vulnerable companies that subsequently blow up or never really recover. After my first ten years of investing, I went through every deal I had made and analysed all the mistakes. By far the most common was buying weakly financed businesses, especially companies with weak cash generation. These accounted for over 75% of the mistakes I had made. That is staggering! Simply paying more attention to financial strength at the time of buying was the stand-out way to improve my results.

It's not just me that highlights the importance of financial strength. All the great value investors – from Anthony Bolton to Warren Buffett – talk about it as a must-have. And the evidence backs them up. As we'll see throughout this chapter, there is a mountain of empirical research from across the globe examining many different definitions of financial strength, and they all come to the same conclusion: no matter how you measure it, strong financial metrics mean better results, *especially* among value shares. With better performance and less volatility, buying financial strength is basically a free lunch.

Why financial strength matters so much

The legendary investor Seth Klarman once summed up value investing as "Buy a bargain and wait." The waiting is as much a part of value investing as the buying. While you're waiting, any number of things can help: sentiment can improve, the cycle can turn, management might make improvements at the company level or make opportunistic share buybacks, and things might improve at the industry level. *Providing the company can afford the wait*, value investing is often like buying an option on a recovery that never expires. Assessing financial strength is really the same as asking: can the company afford the wait?

Companies that do not have sufficiently strong financials are rarely worth buying, even when they may look cheap. The trouble with weak financials is that they can quickly spiral out of control, as happened to many companies and several countries in the global financial crisis of 2007-2009. Financials that might look just about manageable often deteriorate very rapidly as confidence is lost. Then, just as with a bank run, every creditor wants their money back or raises borrowing rates to unbearable levels at the worst possible moment. This is called a death spiral.

Even without a death spiral, weak financials can be bad news. For a start, the company will find it hard to invest in opportunities it should be taking. Most troubled businesses need to undergo serious restructuring, which can be costly. Moreover, under-investing in areas such as research or marketing may permanently damage a company's position. In addition, it may be forced to raise money in ways that damage shareholder value, such as issuing equity or selling off good assets at fire-sale prices. Any or all of these measures will impair the intrinsic value of the company, leaving investors with less than they had hoped.

By contrast, a strongly financed and cash generative business can use difficult periods to create value. It can strengthen its market position by investing in the business or consolidating its position within the industry, just as competitors may be struggling or exiting. And of course it can buy back shares. Buying a really undervalued company with strong financials that is buying back shares is about as close to perfection as you can get. Shareholders can make an awful lot of money out of undervalued companies that are able to do a long series of buybacks.

The two key aspects of financial strength

There are two broad areas the investor must consider in assessing financial strength, both of which are equally critical. The first is solvency, which measures a company's ability to meet its long-term obligations. The second is liquidity, which refers to a company's ability to meets its ongoing cash needs. I'll now look at how to assess solvency and liquidity by using a holistic approach that captures all the important parts.

3.2 Know what you owe

The importance of debt and liabilities

One of the core principles of value investing is thinking like an owner. And if an owner were to look at a business, he would of course consider all the liabilities and obligations as well as the core business, because these are bills which ultimately have to be paid.

Sometimes non-operating assets or liabilities can be so substantial they completely dwarf the core business. In most cases they are at least significant. For this reason, popular price-based measures of valuation (such as P/E or P/S multiples) can be deceptive. To get a true picture of intrinsic value, it is necessary to include a wide range of liabilities (such as debt, provisions or pension obligations) as well as non-operating assets (such as investments and excess cash). This is often referred to as the enterprise value, or EV.

Back-tests comparing the outperformance of low-EV strategies (such as low enterprise value/earnings before interest and taxes (EV/EBIT), low enterprise value/cash flow (EV/CF) and low enterprise value/sales (EV/S) versus their comparable low-price strategies (e.g. low P/E, low price/cash flow (P/CF) or low P/S) have consistently found better performance from the low-EV strategies, illustrating the value of considering the full capital structure.

In addition, low levels of debt or liabilities have also been a good sign in their own right. Many studies have been done around the world comparing debt levels with subsequent share performance.[8] While they

---

8. See for example: Sharaiha, Y., Ekaterina, A., Davidson, R., Funnell, B., Draaisma, T. and Carr, R., 'European Stock Selection – The Factors That Matter' (Morgan Stanley Institutional Equity/Equity Research Europe, December 2002); Sharaiha, Y., Ekaterina, A., Emrich, S., Davidson, R., Funnell, B. and Draaisma, T., 'Stock Selection in the UK – A Comparative Study' (Morgan Stanley Institutional Equity/Equity Research Europe, March 2003); Draaisma, T., Secker, G., Carr, R., Ng, E., Swing, C. and Garman, M., 'Fixed Charge Cover: Another Take on Financial Health', Morgan Stanley Equity Research (Europe, March 2009); Haugen, R. A., *The Inefficient Stock market: What Pays Off and Why* (Prentice Hall, 2001).

have used a wide range of different metrics – such as leverage, gearing and fixed charge cover – they have all reached the same conclusion: those with less debt tend to do significantly better, while those with a lot of liabilities are generally best avoided. This has been especially the case among shares that trade on low multiples.[9]

Surprisingly, the outperformers include those companies sitting on the largest cash piles.[10] Many investors may find this counter-intuitive, and would consider this wasteful when compared to companies that employ optimal gearing strategies. However, in practice it seems the benefits of having that extra cushion are underappreciated.

What makes the case against leverage so compelling is that much of this evidence has been gathered over the past two or three decades – a period during which credit has been cheaper and more freely available than at any time in history. If lavish use of debt cannot help companies outperform during this environment, then it never will!

It is not just the absolute levels of debt and liabilities that matter, but also the trend. Many studies have found that rising levels of debt portend underperformance, while companies paying down their debt tend to outperform.[11] A big part of the problem is that companies tend to gear up at exactly the wrong time. This is because managements are likely to feel most confident and credit tends to be easily available just as a cycle is nearing its peak. Equally, by the time companies have

---

9. See for example: Oppenheimer, H. R., 'A Test of Ben Graham's Stock Selection Criteria', *Financial Analysts Journal* 40:5 (1984), pp. 68-74; study by Tweedy, Browne Company LLC of unleveraged low P/B companies from 1970-1981, reported in *What Has Worked in Investing: Studies of Investment Approaches and Characteristics Associated with Exceptional Returns* (Tweedy, Browne Company LLC, Revised Edition 2009); Draaisma, T., Secker, G., Carr, R., Ng, E., Swing, C. and Garman, M., 'European Strategy: The Unemotional Investor' (Morgan Stanley Equity Research Europe, May 2007).

10. See for example: Goldstein, M. L., Cho, B. J. and Price, N., 'Deeds, Not Words: Capital Deployment, Financing and Their Consequences. Surprisingly, Cash Is Not Trash' (Empirical Research Partners LLC, February 2004).

11. *Ibid.*

reined in their expansion plans and are well into paying down their debt, the cycle is probably approaching the trough.

So the conclusion is this: when looking at value shares, be sure to consider all the company's liabilities. Generally, low levels of debt and liabilities are a good sign, as is falling debt. The converse should be a cause for concern.

Measures of debt and liabilities

Having ascertained that it is important to know a company's levels of debt and liabilities, I'll now look at some ways to measure this.

Gearing

The gearing ratio (net debt/total equity, expressed as a percentage) is commonly used. It is most useful for heavy industries where tangible equity usually reflects the business' worth. It is less relevant for asset-light companies where much of the value is intangible or reflected as goodwill. While there are no hard-and-fast rules, gearing levels above 50% may be a cause for concern, unless the business is very stable – for example some utility companies can carry higher levels than this.

Leverage

The leverage ratio (net debt/earnings before interest, taxes, depreciation and amortization (EBITDA)) can be used for both asset-heavy and asset-light businesses. Once again, there are no hard and fast rules, although lower is clearly better. Generally, levels above 2x should be a cause for concern, unless the business is especially stable.

Fixed charge cover

Fixed charge cover (EBIT + annual rental costs/rental + interest costs) measures how comfortably the company can meet its ongoing interest and rental obligations. Higher is clearly better and anything below two or three may be cause for concern.

Cover is especially important for businesses with a lot of leases, like retailers. Many retailers with seemingly strong balance sheets have been bankrupted by onerous lease obligations. Often these leases run for decades and rise automatically, making it impossible for the company to adapt its business or close loss-making stores. Onerous leases are a common cause of value traps. It is good practice to always check the notes to the accounts for lease obligations, and to consider both the magnitude and duration of those obligations.

Full enterprise value

A fully-adjusted enterprise value is a good way to find out how much you're really paying for the core business. Generally, quoted EVs will only adjust for net debt and minorities, so it is necessary to go through the balance sheet and notes to the accounts to get a more detailed number. Table 3.1 gives a list of some things to look for:

For a full EV add up...	And deduct...
Fully diluted market cap	Cash and equivalents (excluding customer pre-payments)
Minority interests	Investments
Preferred shares	Other non-operating assets (such as excess real estate)
Debt	
Unfunded pension obligations	
Most provisions	
Any potential significant litigation and other significant contingent liabilities	
Net derivative liabilities	

Table 3.1. Things to look for when calculating EV

The above list is not exhaustive. The thing to remember is the principle behind enterprise value, which is to find out what you're paying for the core operating business.

Generally speaking, an EV that is roughly equal to or lower than the market cap is a reassuring sign; while one should be wary of companies where the full EV is substantially higher than the market cap. Such a large amount of liabilities may make the company vulnerable, and price-based measures (such as yield or P/E multiples) are unlikely to give a true reflection of intrinsic value.

3.3 Liquidity

Liquidity is not one specific ratio, but an assessment of several factors to determine a company's ability to meet its ongoing cash needs.

Analysing and monitoring the liquidity positions of holdings is an absolute must.

Liquidity is at least as important as balance sheet strength. One of the most common mistakes among value investors is to assume things are okay because the balance sheet looks fine, while liquidity is deteriorating. This is the classic value trap and sooner or later a liquidity crisis will become a solvency crisis as the company burns through those reserves. Moreover, poor or weakening liquidity is usually the first sign of trouble to come. Being aware of this helps astute investors avoid fragile businesses or get out of them before things turn ugly.

Assessing liquidity

I will now run through the most important measures of liquidity. As with solvency, investors should not just focus on absolute numbers, but also their directions.

Cash flows and operating profitability

Cash flows are by far the most important element to consider when assessing liquidity. Companies need cash to carry on operating and companies that cannot make real money are at best worthless. At worst they can suck in more funds for years and squander them.

Companies with strong liquidity positions will generally have histories of consistently positive operating cash flows and free cash flows. As well as the history, the outlook for cash flows must also be considered: be wary if they are falling or if operating profits have collapsed.

Cash flow measures are generally a better measure than earnings. Real cash flow is harder to manipulate. A very common sign in troubled companies is that cash flows fall faster than earnings as working capital builds up. So if cash flows are deteriorating, check for a rapid build-up of inventories or receivables. This is almost always a harbinger of worse things to come.

Working capital and the current ratio

The current ratio (current assets/current liabilities) should generally be well above 1, indicating the company has more assets it expects to monetise over the next year than liabilities it has to meet. There are certain examples of negative working capital businesses (such as supermarkets), which only have to pay their suppliers after the goods are sold, and can therefore run safely with lower current ratios. However, generally a current ratio of around or below 1 is a cause for concern.

Cash and undrawn facilities

For a company to be able to operate comfortably, it should have a decent cushion of cash on the balance sheet, and perhaps some undrawn credit facilities as well. Undrawn credit facilities are the corporate equivalent of overdraft facilities, allowing companies to dip into them when needed. Obviously the more the better, but the expiry dates and covenants on the facilities (the conditions the company must meet to use them) are also relevant.

Refinancing needs

Refinancing needs refers to when the company's outstanding debt expires and has to be paid back or refinanced. Ideally these should be spread over a long period with a small portion maturing each year. A company with a lot of debt maturing in a short period may have difficulty attracting the funds it needs to refinance, particularly if its operating environment or the economy is having difficulties at the same time.

3.4 General measures of financial strength

There are several broad measures of financial strength which incorporate many of the indicators discussed above. These can provide useful additional checks.

Bond ratings and reports

Where companies have bonds outstanding, the bond markets and rating agencies (such as Fitch, S&P and Moody's) monitor and analyse the debt position. Rating agencies and debt markets are often quicker than stock markets to identify funding problems or improvements. Getting hold of ratings and credit reports is a helpful starting point and will address most of the areas discussed in the previous sections.

Piotroski Scores (F-Scores)

In a landmark study,[12] Joseph Piotroski demonstrated the value of adding a range of financial strength measures to a traditional value approach.

---

12. Piotroski, J. D., 'Value Investing: The Use of Historical Financial

The finance professor had noticed that the performance of value strategies was being dragged down by firms with weak financials. So he devised a nine-factor F-Score for assessing balance sheet strength and liquidity. The nine factors are:

1. net income > 0

2. operating cash flow > 0

3. operating cash flow > net income

4. total debt/total assets has fallen over the previous year

5. working capital (current assets - current liabilities) is higher than previous year

6. asset turnover (revenues/total assets) is higher than the previous year

7. return on assets is higher than the previous year

8. shares outstanding is less than or equal to last year's total

9. gross profit margin is higher than the previous year

Companies are awarded one point for each of the nine criteria that they meet, and a score of 7 to 9 is considered good.

The actual study (covering US shares from 1976 to 1996) bought companies with price/book ratios of below 1.5 and with an F-Score of 7 or more. The companies chosen outperformed by an average of 7.5% per annum, with results especially strong among small caps. This is far superior to a simple low valuation strategy, and the annual returns are more consistent.

Subsequent studies have affirmed Piotroski's original findings, both in the US and abroad.[13]

Statement Information to Separate Winners from Losers', *Journal of Accounting Research* 38 Supplement (2000).

13. Goldstein, M. L. and Cho, B., 'Finding Small-Capitalization Turnaround Situations That Work' (Empirical Research Partners LLC, June 2003); Draaisma, T., Secker, G., Carr, R., Ng, E., Swing, C. and Garman, M., 'Euroletter: A Health Check for Corporate Balance Sheets' (Morgan Stanley Equity Research Europe, July 2008).

It is particularly striking that not all of the nine factors are of equal importance. Indeed, about 90% of the total outperformance from the F-score comes from just one of the nine factors, which is operating cash flow over the previous 12 months. This should be positive.[14] This illustrates how important positive cash generation is for value shares.

Chart 3.1 of Joseph Piotroski's results illustrates the benefits of focusing on cheap stocks with financial strength. The outperformance of this segment is dramatic; while cheap stocks with weak financial positions underperform significantly.

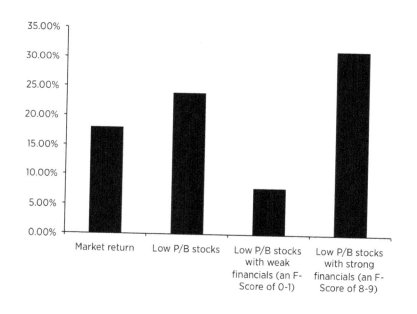

Chart 3.1. Outperformance of cheap stocks with financial strength

---

14. Piotroski, J. D., 'Value Investing: The Use of Historical Financial Statement Information to Separate Winners from Losers', *Journal of Accounting Research* 38:Supplement (2000); Goldstein, M. L. and Cho, B., 'Finding Small-Capitalization Turnaround Situations That Work' (Empirical Research Partners LLC, June 2003).

Altman Z-Scores

The Z-Score was developed in the 1960s by Edward Altman as a formula for predicting bankruptcy. By incorporating five factors related to profitability, liquidity and liabilities, it can provide a valuable snapshot of overall financial health.

The Z-Score formula is:

Z-Score = 1.2 x (working capital/total assets) + 1.4 x (retained earnings/total assets) + 3.3 x (EBIT/total assets) + 0.6 x (market value of equity/book value of liabilities) + 1 x (sales/total assets)

The higher the Z-Score the better. A general rule is that anything below 1.5 is getting a bit hairy, and anything above 3 is super-safe. But there are anomalies in certain industries, so a comparison with similar companies may be more appropriate. Some financial information providers (e.g. Bloomberg) calculate Z-Scores, which can save you a lot of time.

Over the years, the Z-Score has built a distinguished record for spotting companies early on that may later become distressed. Avoiding companies with Z-Scores below 1 has been especially effective.[15]

The Z-Score is far from perfect and needs to be considered alongside other factors, but it provides another quick check that can help to avoid trouble later on.

---

15. Draaisma, T., Secker, G., Carr, R., Ng, E., Swing, C. and Garman, M., 'Euroletter: A Health Check for Corporate Balance Sheets' (Morgan Stanley Equity Research Europe, July 2008).

3.5 Summary

- Paying attention to financial strength is the most effective way to avoid value traps. Value shares with strong financials make far better investments than those with weak financials.

- Be holistic: no single measure is enough. Demand both strong solvency and strong liquidity.

- Having said that, the record and outlook for cash generation is probably the most important single measure in assessing financial strength.

- Don't just focus on the current numbers: look out for improving or deteriorating trends in financial metrics.

- In assessing valuation, a full EV (enterprise value) measure is more useful than market-cap based measures. Similarly, when devising screens or search strategies, use EV-based multiples rather than price-based multiples.

- In addition, add financial strength requirements to screens (e.g. cash flow > 0, gearing < 50%, etc.) alongside value metrics. It is all too easy to get lured into a value trap by a very low valuation, so take value traps out of sight!

- There is a wide range of factors that need to be considered in assessing financial strength, so make a financial strength checklist to ensure you don't miss out any of them (there's more on creating checklists in Chapter 9).

- A summary of good and bad signs of financial strength is given in Table 3.2.

Good signs	Bad signs
Little debt. Falling debt (low leverage/low gearing/high cover).	Lots of debt. Rising debt (high leverage/high gearing/low cover).
Well covered lease obligations, ideally with a short duration.	Large and onerous lease commitments.
Strong or improving cash flows and operating profits. (Especially important.)	Weak, negative or deteriorating cash flows and operating profits. (Especially important.)
A healthy cash and cash equivalents balance in relation to market cap and a comfortable current ratio.	Little cash and equivalents on the balance sheet, or an unusually low current ratio for that type of business.
Low levels of other liabilities, both on and off-balance sheet.	Other large debt-like commitments, both on and off-balance sheet.

Table 3.2. Good and bad signs of financial strength

CHAPTER 4

Invest Like an Owner

4.1 Ownership and alignment

Stewardship is critical to value investors because it has an enormous effect on intrinsic value. If the business' assets are misused or stolen, or the reported numbers are not real, any assessment of the business' worth becomes almost impossible. In the worst of such instances, no price is too cheap.

Unfortunately, some 'value' shares are dreadfully managed, while others are outright frauds. This is more common than one might imagine. In recent years, irresponsible or fraudulent management has proved a big problem for many value investors, and especially some large quant funds.

The number of ways unscrupulous managements can steal from or deceive shareholders is infinite. What makes things more difficult still is that it is all but impossible for an outside shareholder to closely supervise every management action, let alone do anything about it.

The importance of responsible stewardship has increased with the globalisation of investing and the increasing significance of emerging markets. Many of these countries – most notably Russia, India and China – do not have the same shareholder protections and rule of law enjoyed in most developed markets. While there are many attractive investment opportunities in these places, one has to be even more careful.

By contrast, however, incredible opportunities continue to emerge where there is good stewardship and close alignment with shareholders. Often these involve stunning turnarounds of deeply troubled businesses. It is amazing what people can achieve with ingenuity and hard work when they are incentivised to do so.

As with financial strength, there is no single factor with which to assess ownership and alignment. Instead, it is necessary to take a mosaic approach and consider many different elements piece-by-piece. Often it quickly becomes apparent that a company has many positive features and is worth consideration. In other instances there will be lots of red flags and the company should be avoided.

Basic ownership factors

I have provided a summary of the basic ownership factors to look out for below.

Concentrated stakes among active owners

Companies where management or commercially-minded investors have large stakes have tended to deliver superior long-term performance.[16]

---

16. See for example: Draaisma, T., Secker, G., Carr, R., Ng, E., Swing, C. and Garman, M., 'European Strategy: Dusting Off The Family Jewels' (Morgan Stanley Equity Research Europe, September 2007); Miller, K. L., 'Best of the Best', (*Newsweek*, April 2004); 'Shut up and get rich', *Investors Chronicle* (August 2003); Poutziouris, P., 'The UK Family Business PLC Economy', Institute for Family Business UK, London (2006); Gugler, K., Mueller, D. C. and Yurtoglu, B. B., 'The Impact of Corporate Governance on Investment Returns in Developed and Developing Countries', *The Economic Journal* 113 (November 2003); Anderson, R. C. and Reeb, D. M., 'Who Monitors the Family?' (2003), available at SSRN: ssrn.com/abstract=369620; Grabowski, H. G. and Mueller, D. C., 'Life-Cycle Effects on Corporate Returns on

The evidence suggests owner-managed companies outperform because they take a long-term approach to decision-making, avoid excessive leverage, prefer focus over diversification, and are more disciplined with capital (investing less and at higher rates of return, and giving more back to shareholders).[17]

Be aware, however, that not all large stakeholders may be a positive. Governments or parent companies may have agendas of their own which are inimical to those of minority shareholders, so it is important to consider the motivations and past behaviour of these groups.

Insider buying

This is where those involved in the management of the company or those with large stakes who are close to the company buy up shares in the open market. In most countries, insider purchases have to be reported. Once again there is a lot of evidence that companies seeing heavy insider buying tend to outperform subsequently.[18]

This is not surprising. Like anyone else, there is only one reason why insiders buy shares – they think they're going up. But unlike anyone else, insiders are often in a better position to judge when to buy the shares.

While buying shares based on knowledge of specific events not yet announced would count as illegal insider dealing, management are likely to possess more general *insight information*. That is, they will

Retentions', *The Review of Economics and Statistics* 57:4 (1975), pp. 400-409.

17. See for example: Draaisma, T., Secker, G., Carr, R., Ng, E., Swing, C. and Garman, M., 'European Strategy: Dusting Off The Family Jewels' (Morgan Stanley Equity Research Europe, September 2007).

18. See for example: Glass, G. S., 'Extensive Insider Accumulation as an Indicator of Near Term Stock Price Performance', PhD Diss. (Ohio State University, 1966); Rogoff, D. L., 'The Forecasting Properties of Insiders' Transactions', *The Journal of Finance* 19:4 (1964), pp. 697-698; Devere, C. W., 'Relationship Between Insider Trading and Future Performance of NYSE Common Stocks 1960-1965', Diss. (Portland State College, 1968); Jaffe, J. F., 'Special Information and Insider Trading', *The Journal of Business* 47:3 (1974), pp. 410-428; Zweig, M. E., 'Canny Insiders: Their Transactions Give a Clue to Market Performance' (*Barrons*. July 1976); King, M. and Roell, A., 'Insider Trading', *Economic Policy* 3:6 (1988), pp. 163-193.

know about things like the potential of new products, big contracts, hidden assets or cost-cutting options. Additionally, insiders tend to have a long-term perspective on the business, so they often buy when they judge the market to be overly depressed about the company's prospects.

Insider transactions can be particularly valuable in complex or opaque businesses. No one else is likely to be able to judge the prospects as well as management, so insider buying can make up for imperfect information.

Not all insider buys are equally useful. It is important to consider who is buying, how often and how much. A purchase by an executive director in charge of the day-to-day running of the company is likely to be a more significant signal than a non-executive who may be employed on a consultative role. Generally, several insiders making large or repeat purchases is a more positive signal than just one or two purchases of a token amount.

Chart 4.1 of Dawson Geophysical (an oil services company) shows how canny insiders bought in opportunistically during the financial crisis, before selling down when prices and sentiment recovered. You can obtain a useful snapshot of the record of insiders' share dealings such as this using the Insider Transactions function on Bloomberg.

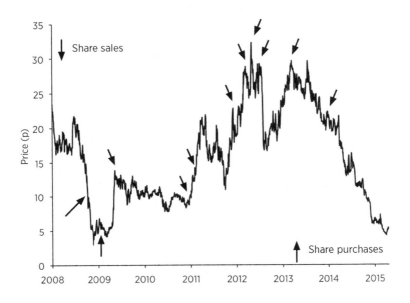

Chart 4.1. Dawson Geophysical management buying and selling

Shareholder returns (dividends and buybacks)

Dividends and buybacks tend to be positive signals for future share performance. Shareholder returns demonstrate that a company is making real money, is keen to reward its shareholders, and is confident about its current financial position and prospects. Buybacks are especially effective amongst lowly valued shares, as buying back undervalued shares creates more value for remaining shareholders.[19]

---

19. Funnell, B., Draaisma, T., Secker, G., Carr, R. and Bostrom, D., 'Buy Buybacks' (Morgan Stanley Equity Research Europe, June 2004); Bali, T. G., Demirtas, K. O. and Hovakimian, A., 'Corporate Financing Activities and Contrarian Investment', *Review of Finance* 14:3 (2010), pp. 543-584; Goldstein M. and Cho, B., 'Corporate Cash Flow, Debt and Dividend Policy: Analysis and Implications for Stock Selection' (Empirical Research Partners LLC, June 2003).

Equally, it is generally wise to avoid companies that are constantly raising financing or issuing more and more shares, as they tend to make very poor investments. If a company is *very* cheap and it is neither buying back shares nor seeing insider buying, that can be almost a red flag in itself.

4.2 Look for evidence of capital discipline

Capital discipline refers to how carefully a company's management uses the capital available to it. Some management teams are incredibly disciplined and spend very cautiously, keeping costs low and paying out generous amounts to shareholders. Others are very aggressive, throwing money at myriad projects, buying up other businesses, and raising capital at every opportunity. Most common, however, are capital cycles, with management oscillating between aggressive and cautious as the outlook changes.

There is overwhelming evidence that companies adopting a disciplined approach to spending tend to perform much better than those acting aggressively.[20] Value investors should therefore try to identify companies with a long record of disciplined capital allocation, or at least companies that are deep into the disciplined part of their capital cycle. There are a number of things to look out for and I have described these below.

---

20. Goldstein, M. L., Cho, B. J. and Price, N., 'Deeds, Not Words: Capital Deployment, Financing and Their Consequences. Surprisingly, Cash Is Not Trash' (Empirical Research Partners LLC, February 2004); Adrian, S., Yang, S. and Sapp, W., 'International Portfolio Strategy: Emerging Market Modelling (Part II): Using Capital Deployment and Earnings Quality to Pick Stocks' (Empirical Research Partners LLC, October 2009); Goldstein, M. L., Cho, B. J., Price, N. and Dix, L., 'The Small-Capitalization Value Stock Selection Model. Trust, But Verify' (Empirical Research Partners LLC, November 2004).

Cost cutting or tight cost controls

Most companies are at least a bit inefficient, but it is easy for some corporations to squander billions just through a lax attitude to costs. Additionally, sloppy cost controls are usually a sign of hubristic management, or nearing the peak of a cycle.

Companies with rapidly growing operating costs tend to underperform in the years that follow, while those displaying the lowest cost growth tend to outperform.[21] Look for management teams that keep a tight control on operating costs and take out costs where they can. Avoid management teams that appear profligate: new headquarters, private jets, vanity projects or excessively generous salaries are all things to watch for.

Generous shareholder returns or debt paydown

As we shall see in more detail later on (section 5.4), shareholder returns and/or paying down debt are valuable signs of capital discipline. By contrast, growing debt (especially convertible debt) and/or aggressive share issuance usually portend trouble.[22] Again, indiscipline tends to signal a peak in the cycle, and may also reflect management's view that the company's shares are overvalued (financially, it makes sense for a company to issue more shares when they are overvalued).

Little or no M&A

While deal-making can seem glamorous, deals are normally much better for the target than the acquirer. Indeed, evidence shows that significant deal-making is one of the worst forms of capital allocation,

---

21. Huang, D., Jiang, F., Tu, J. and Guofu, Z., 'Cost Growth and Stock Returns' (2014), available at SSRN: ssrn.com/abstract=2460540.
22. Goldstein, M. L., Cho, B. J. and Price, N., 'Deeds, Not Words: Capital Deployment, Financing and Their Consequences. Surprisingly, Cash Is Not Trash' (Empirical Research Partners LLC, February 2004); Lee, I. and Loughran, T., 'Performance following convertible bond issuance', *Journal of Corporate Finance* 4:2 (1998), pp. 185-207.

with over two-thirds of deals destroying shareholder value, and the acquirer underperforming for years afterwards.[23]

The reasons for this are that managements usually do deals near the top of the cycle and overpay for them. They also tend to underestimate the practical difficulties of bringing two separate companies together, such as cultural differences or the amount of restructuring required.

In summary, be very sceptical of companies doing large deals, or doing lots of deals. Be especially wary of deals paid for in shares or where the deals diversify the business away from its core.

Subdued levels of capex and working capital

As companies tend to spend heavily on capex at the wrong point in the cycle, it is normally wise to avoid them when they are investing heavily in capex.[24] Rapidly growing working capital (inventories and receivables) can also be a negative signal, as it suggests the company is producing more than its customers want.[25]

---

23. See for example: 'Capital Use: R&D, Patents and Acquisitions' (Bernstein Research, December 2001); Sirower, M. L., *The Synergy Trap: How Companies Lose the Acquisition Game* (Simon & Schuster, 1997); Loughran, T. and Vijh, A. M., 'Do Long-Term Shareholders Benefit From Corporate Acquisitions?', *Journal of Finance* 52:5 (1997), pp. 1765-1790; Mitchell, M. L. and Stafford, E., 'Managerial Decisions and Long-Term Stock Price Performance', *Journal of Business* 73:3 (2000), pp 287-329; Goldstein, M. L., Cho, B. J. and Price, N., 'Deeds, Not Words: Capital Deployment, Financing and Their Consequences. Surprisingly, Cash Is Not Trash' (Empirical Research Partners LLC, February 2004).

24. Goldstein, M. L., Cho, B. J. and Price, N., 'Capital Spending Is Growing Again: Implications For Stock Selection. Convertible Bond Issuance: Dilution For Sale' (Empirical Research Partners LLC, March 2004); Goldstein, M. L., Cho, B. J., Price, N. and Dix, L., 'Capital Spending and Its Consequences: Triumph of the Optimists?' (Empirical Research Partners LLC, October 2004); Siegel, J. J., *The Future for Investors: Why the Tried and True Triumph Over the Bold and the New* (New York: Crown Business, 2005).

25. Goldstein, M. L., Cho, B. J. and Price, N., 'Exploiting Earnings Quality to Identify Winning and Losing Stocks' (Empirical Research Partners LLC, March 2004).

Inventory build-up occurs when a company makes more products than it sells. Receivables build-up occurs where a company is increasingly extending credit to customers so they do not have to pay till later – this is called *channel stuffing*.

A record of high returns on capital

A long record of sound capital discipline will normally be evident from a company's ten- or 20-year record of returns on capital. Consistently high returns on capital are achieved by only investing in very profitable opportunities.

A record of countercyclical spending

Companies that manage to invest counter-cyclically over a long period are extremely rare and are almost always run by owners with large stakes. Countercyclical spending involves investing heavily during severe downturns, and then saving up during boom times. Some companies get lucky and time a cycle correctly, but it takes extreme discipline to do this consistently. If you can find such behaviour in a company, this is highly valuable.

4.3 Due diligence

Due diligence refers to the process of carefully investigating a company before buying it, to make sure you're getting what you think you're getting. How much due diligence is required depends a lot on the company. A large, reputable business with a sound financial record going back decades requires far less than, say, an obscure emerging market business that has only been listed for a year or two.

Thorough due diligence involves checking a wide range of factors. Rather than looking for things to confirm the investment case, the purpose of due diligence is to look for signs of potential trouble. These are often called *red flags*.

There are many potential red flags to look out for (a summary checklist is provided in section 4.4). Examples include things like qualified or late accounts, suspicious or complex related party transactions between the company and other entities, executives with murky backgrounds, or rapidly growing working capital. Generally it is best to walk away from a share where there are multiple or very serious red flags.

Internet searches are often a helpful and quick due diligence tool. Googling the names of executives, general articles on the company and investor blogs often throws up some valuable results. Local contacts can also be useful, especially if the company operates a long way away. Ask local acquaintances if they are familiar with the products or know anyone who works for the company. Additionally, if you have access to local brokers or analysts, it is worthwhile speaking to them privately (often they will tell you things that they would not say on the record).

Once again, one of the best tools for due diligence is the record of cash flow statements. Companies that fail to generate real operating cash flows or persistently raise capital are almost always the ones that turn out to be deeply troubled or fraudulent.

Cash from financing: the Cinderella of accounts analysis

One of my favourite parts of a company's accounts is *cash from financing*. It is very helpful when carrying out due diligence. While the income statement and the balance sheet tend to get lots of attention, the cash flow statement often gets neglected. Yet for many of the most successful investors, the cash flow statement is the part they pay most attention to. It is much harder to manipulate than the income statements and reflects the true cash the company is making or losing.

Cash from financing is the third part of the cash flow statement (even more neglected than the operating cash flow and investing cash flow sections that come above it). It is also the hardest part of the financial statements to manipulate or lie about. This is because it is predominantly made up of the cash that is raised from or paid to debt holders and shareholders – the very people who read the financial statements!

So it's no surprise that almost every incident of fraud or serious mismanagement around the world has been accompanied by a long record of positive cash from financing (meaning the company has had to keep going to lenders or shareholders for more money). By contrast, as we have already seen, companies that are paying out real cash to their owners or lenders tend to make for happier investments.

4.4 Summary

- Many seemingly cheap shares are badly managed and some are outright frauds. Take the time to assess ownership and alignment, the record of capital discipline and shareholder returns, as well as due diligence factors.

- A mosaic approach is required. No company is perfectly good or perfectly bad, but by looking at many indicators an overall pattern should become clear.

- The cash flow statement (and especially cash from financing) is especially useful for due diligence and assessing capital discipline.

- The three tables below provide checklists for: ownership and alignment; capital discipline; and due diligence.

Ownership and alignment checks

Good signs	Bad signs
Significant stakes among management and commercially-minded or activist shareholders.	Large holdings among those whose interests are not well aligned with those of minority shareholders. Especially where there is a history of actions that have hurt minorities in the past.
Management or large holders buying shares in the open market.	Insider selling can be a negative signal, although there may be other non-commercial motivations for a sale.
Record of decent shareholder returns and capital discipline (see below).	Record of capital raising and heavy spending (see below).

Capital discipline checks

Signs of disciplined capital allocation (good)	Signs of wasteful capital allocation (bad)
Subdued levels of capital expenditure.	Elevated levels of capital expenditure.
Paying growing or consistent dividends and/or buying back shares.	Failing to pay out dividends or to buy back shares, even when profitable. Also, be wary of dividends that are not covered by cash flows or paid for by issuing equity. Issuing new shares or significant amounts of dilutive securities (e.g. convertible bonds).
Low and/or falling levels of debt, or net cash.	Consistently high or rising levels of debt.

Signs of disciplined capital allocation (good)	Signs of wasteful capital allocation (bad)
No M&A; or a few small, bolt-on deals only.	Aggressive M&A. Be especially wary of large deals, diversifying deals, deals paid for with shares, deals paying high multiples or deals buying into popular industries.
Signs of good cost control and a focus on costs.	Profligacy, such as private jets, fancy headquarters, vanity projects, etc.
Working capital (especially inventory days and days receivable) at normal or subdued levels.	Ballooning working capital.
A long record of consistently high returns on capital or countercyclical investing.	Low returns or signs that the company is spending heavily late in the capital cycle.
A record of negative cash from financing.	A record of positive cash from financing.

Due diligence: potential red flags

Vulnerable business models to be wary of	• Consumer fads • Serial acquirers/aggressively diversifying • Complex businesses or structures • New/recent IPOs • Financial or real estate companies • Franchise models • Highly leveraged companies • Cash guzzlers that cannot self-fund • Very fast growing companies

Weak funding	• Weak or negative operating cash flows • Persistent cash burn (negative free cash flow) • High/growing debt • Repeatedly requiring more funding (record of positive cash from financing) • Exotic securities issuance (e.g. convertible debt, warrants, PIK notes, etc.) • Low or negative returns on capital
Capital indiscipline	• High total asset growth • Growth in days receivable (especially long-term or unbilled receivables) • Growth in inventory days • Growth in prepaid expenses and other current assets
Misleading balance sheet	• Large off-balance sheet liabilities (e.g. litigation, leases, purchase commitments) • Mark-to-model accounting (often used by companies in the financial sector)
Poor earnings quality	• Sales booked aggressively • Large capitalised expenses (R&D, software, marketing costs, etc.) in the balance sheet • Deferred charges • Unusually long or altered depreciation rates • Income boosted by one-time gains or non-core activities • Operating cash flow less than net income
Stewardship issues	• High executive pay and generous perks (e.g. fees, options, loans, big severance packages) • Aggressive options issuance • Large or complex related party transactions • Insider selling • Firing auditors (opinion shopping) • Accounts are qualified or filed late • Lack of independent directors (lots of relatives in key jobs – look for the same surname!) • Aggressive M&A • High management turnover/departure of key personnel

CHAPTER 5

Better Valuation

5.1 Absolute value is what counts

Absolute value, or intrinsic value, involves estimating the future cash flows a business can make (even if this is just a matter of liquidating the assets) and valuing them against your required rate of return. This approach is not concerned with the market valuation or the rates of return other investors may be using.

By contrast, relative valuation involves comparing the valuation metrics of a company with its peers or the wider market. Here, a company would be viewed as undervalued if those metrics were cheaper than the relevant peers.

The whims of the market can have a great effect on relative valuations, so true value investing is mostly concerned with intrinsic value. At the core of value investing is the notion of acting as a private owner would – that is, independently of the market. In order to do this effectively, you first need to have an idea of what the business is worth. Once you have this, it will tell you when to buy and when to sell, as well as providing the confidence to exploit any volatility in the meantime.

Without valuation, no reasonable decisions can be made, nor will it be possible to identify the attractiveness of an opportunity relative to another.

From the simple disciplines of absolute valuation and margin of safety, all other qualities required for successful investing spring forth: patience, low turnover, good buy and sell discipline, and long-term thinking. Moreover, if you focus on absolute valuations and then buy the best bargains, in the long run relative returns will look after themselves.

The dangers of relying on relative valuation

While simply buying relatively cheaply valued shares will generally beat more expensive shares, it will not in itself guarantee a good profit.

This is because in times of exuberance, relatively cheap shares can still be overvalued. For example, buying 'cheap' Japanese shares in the late 1980s still meant paying 40 or 50 times earnings, as did buying 'cheap' tech shares in the tech bubble. In excessive markets, relative valuation does not provide protection against losing money.

Relative value investors also run into problems during periods when market valuations converge, as happened in the so-called *dash-for-trash*, from about 2005 to 2007. In this environment, investors became obsessed with relative valuation with little regard for business quality, prospects, financial strength or management. The result is that vulnerable businesses get bid up to levels only just below great businesses. At these times, you're much better paying a little more for something a lot better and a lot more valuable (this is discussed in more detail later). Only by making a proper assessment of intrinsic value that takes account of the qualities and risks that are specific to the individual business will this become clear.

For similar reasons, relative valuations among peers can also be misleading. For example, a comparison across the media sector could make a highly profitable and growing online franchise look expensive compared to a rapidly declining newspaper company with enormous pension liabilities. Or an oil company run by crooks in a country where corruption and expropriation are rife might trade at a large discount to oil companies in safer places and with proven records of generating shareholder value, yet the former may be worth nothing at all.

Further, spot multiples used in relative valuations can often be deceptive themselves. Spot valuations typically only reflect one year's results, so they may tell you nothing about the future. A company may have a blow-out year or a terrible year that may never be repeated again, meaning those results will not give a true sense of what is normal.

A final, but very important, problem with relative valuation is that it can lead to more speculative and herd-like approaches. By comparing to the market, it is all too easy to become more like the market, and focus too much on Mr Market's short-term whims and less on the true value of the underlying businesses.

All in all, the standard of absolute valuation is much higher than that of relative valuation. It requires more diligence and offers far fewer opportunities. True value investors have to look harder and often go further, to the most neglected corners of the world. Their reward is higher returns and more consistent returns.

The importance of not reaching

One of the difficulties with using absolute valuation is that the number of opportunities available will vary enormously. In very depressed markets you may be overwhelmed with appealing investments, but in booming markets you may not be able to find enough to fill your portfolio, or you may have to look much harder.

During these periods of exuberance, it is tempting to start *reaching* for ideas. By this I mean tweaking your normal standards and assumptions to make opportunities look more valuable. This can happen inadvertently – you may not even realise you are being more aggressive than usual.

What drives this urge to reach is the influence of Mr Market's emotions on your own behaviour and especially the fear of missing out while others around you get rich. This is the fear that drives all speculative bubbles.

Yet it is exactly what you must avoid. The time to overlook imperfections or even to dream up rosy scenarios is when things have been collapsing for a good while and everyone else is running for the exits. In times of optimism, the default must remain, "No thank you."

It is important to remember that missing out on a bargain now and again as a result of being overly conservative is not really a problem, because sooner or later you are sure to find another one. Conversely, if you do overpay, you not only lose money, but you lose the future opportunity to invest that money in a genuine bargain.

This highly disciplined approach will often force you into looking beyond your normal hunting ground and into the least popular places. This is no bad thing: there is plenty of evidence demonstrating how buying into the cheapest sectors and countries delivers superior long-run returns.

Absolute value is the ultimate circuit-breaker

As well as enforcing better buy discipline, absolute valuation enforces better sell discipline, as the same valuation will indicate when it is time to sell. Valuation serves as both entry strategy and exit strategy.

The legendary American financier, John Pierpont Morgan, once quipped, "I made my fortune by getting out too soon." His point is invaluable: markets tend to swing too far both ways, and you are never going to get out right at the top. Simply selling well is enough, even for a billionaire.

Now and again different shares and different investment approaches become wildly popular. At these times it is easy for an investor to get caught up in the euphoria, especially as he sees enormous paper profits piling up. As J. K. Galbraith put it, "Speculation buys up the intelligence of those involved."[26] At these times maximum absolute valuations put in place during a more sober period will boot you out of shares as they become heavily overvalued and pile you into those areas where the opportunities are most compelling.

---

26. Galbraith, J. K., *A Short History of Financial Euphoria* (Penguin Group US, 1994).

Holding cash

On some occasions, there may be insufficient opportunities no matter where you look. This is especially likely when markets are strong across the board and you find yourself selling out of holdings that have become fully valued at a faster rate than you can find replacements. The result is that you end up accumulating cash.

This can feel very uncomfortable in rising markets, as there is that dreadful feeling of missing out while more aggressive investors are making hay. Nevertheless, temporarily accumulating cash in these circumstances is the logical approach. Overvalued markets always swing back sooner or later. When they do, they usually swing too far, offering up a flood of real bargains.

Market history is littered with examples of successful investors building up cash piles in bull markets and then making fabulous returns when they dive back in after a correction. Warren Buffett was forced out of the bull market in the early 1970s and then roared back in to make a fortune as some great bargains emerged. More recently, a few value investors found themselves pushed out in the 2005-2007 dash for trash, and then made a killing picking up bargains in the subsequent collapse. Peter Cundill described this as, "The perfect example of the way the value discipline in action provided a form of inbuilt safety valve."[27]

It is important that holding cash in this way is distinguished from the popular concept of *market timing*. Market timing involves trying to second-guess the market's fluctuations based on factors such as momentum, sentiment and economic considerations, rather than the availability of sufficiently undervalued individual shares. But, as Benjamin Graham emphasised, what matters for the investor is not *when* he buys and sells but *at what price*:

> "Timing does not benefit the investor unless it coincides with pricing... in such a policy, timing and pricing would clearly coincide – he would be buying at the right time because he would be buying at the right price, and vice versa."[28]

27. Risso-Gill, C., *There's Always Something to Do: The Peter Cundill Investment Approach* (McGill-Queen's University Press, 2011).

28. Graham, B., *The Intelligent Investor: A Book of Practical Counsel* (New

How to use relative valuation

For all its flaws, relative valuation does have its uses and serves as a helpful complement to the assessment of intrinsic worth.

Firstly, it serves as a useful sense-check. If your assessment of value is way out of whack with comparable or historic multiples, it may be worth revisiting your assumptions. Moreover, relative valuation can also help identify if a whole sector or market may be worth closer consideration.

Some specific tips when considering relative valuations are:

1. Compare valuations not only with sector peers, but with wider market multiples and with the company's long-run historic multiples.

2. Compare with median multiples, rather than simple averages, as the latter can be skewed by outliers.

3. Make sure you use appropriate measures of valuation. For example, price-to-tangible book value may be useful when looking at heavy industries, such as cement, but is much less relevant for, say, a tech franchise.

4. Compare EV (enterprise value) multiples as well as price multiples, as these take account of the capital structure, especially how much debt the company has.

York: Harper & Row, 1973).

5.2 Not just nearly cheap, but really cheap

"Buy only the best bargains."

Sir John Templeton

Narrow in on the value deciles

As we have seen, while absolute value trumps relative value, relative value still has its uses. Where it is most useful is in terms of idea generation.

There are far too many shares around the world for a large department of people, let alone an individual, to analyse and monitor. What is needed from the start is some tool to whittle that number down – and one of the most helpful tools is to screen based on relative valuation.

This involves screening only for shares in the lowest deciles (i.e. the cheapest 10%) based on valuation measures, such as P/B, P/E, EV/EBIT or EV-to-free cash flow.

Shrinking your universe in this simple way will not only save you a lot of work, but will also add a lot of value. Over recent decades, thousands of back-tests have been done examining the performance of shares based on their valuation metrics. While these studies cover different time periods and geographic regions, almost all of them have found that long-run returns are highest among shares in the cheapest deciles. This result holds no matter whether you use multiples of book value, profits, cash flows or sales.

For example, Chart 5.1 from the Brandes Institute[29] illustrates how much higher long-term global share returns have been for the most

---

29. 'Value Versus Glamour: A Global Phenomenon' (The Brandes Institute, November 2012), available online at www.brandes.com/institute/research.

lowly valued shares. As can be seen, it is right at the extreme end of cheapness that value investing tends to work best.

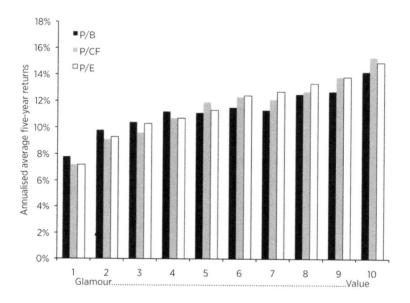

Chart 5.1. Higher long-term global returns from lower valued shares

While it makes sense to focus on the very cheapest decile in practice, most value investors end up plumping for shares that are more in the middle of the range. As we'll see later on, this is because they find it too uncomfortable to buy the ugliest or most neglected businesses. In so doing, they miss out on the real benefits of value investing.

Just because others miss out on the best bargains, it doesn't mean you have to. By employing simple screens to focus your analysis on the cheapest segments of the market, you can make sure you're always looking in the most profitable places.

The importance of big winners

Many value investing approaches have relatively high failure rates, with the strong performance driven by a minority of shares that go up by a very large amount. Thus, it is important to select shares where there really is potential for a big win over the long term.

This is where the margin of safety comes in. For example, always using a 50% margin of safety on top of a conservative valuation will ensure there is the likelihood of, at the very least, doubling your money in every investment.

Demanding so much upside will make many value shares seem a lot less attractive. For example, one might find a share that is holding its market cap in cash, but the operating business may not be worth much at all (and the cash may get squandered or sit idle for years), so even though EV measures may appear very low, there isn't actually much upside.

The same goes for many low quality, low price-to-book (P/B) shares. For example, a low-quality business on 0.7x book isn't that cheap if its true worth is, say, 0.8x to 0.9x.

5.3 Be flexible

To everything there is a season in investing. There are times to be in bonds, times to be in blue chips, times for real estate and times for emerging markets. Different investments and approaches cycle in and out of fashion. And so it is with value investing.

As we have seen, there are many different valuation techniques that can be used for different types of business, and there are equally as many different screens and search approaches to find attractive shares. At different times, some of these techniques work far better than others. Generally, low price-to-sales (P/S) and low price-to-book (P/B) approaches will uncover the best opportunities in deep bear markets after steep cyclical downturns, as they identify the shares with the most to gain from a recovery in profitability. However, in late-stage bull markets, strategies focusing on operating stability and shareholder yields are more fruitful thanks to their downside protection.

It is therefore important to use a range of valuation techniques and screens. Moreover, the willingness and ability to consider many different situations will enable you to look widely and without prejudice. Prejudice among investors as a whole is often the best source of opportunity for value investors. This occurs when the investment community shuns a whole area because of uncertainty, ugly headlines or just misunderstanding.

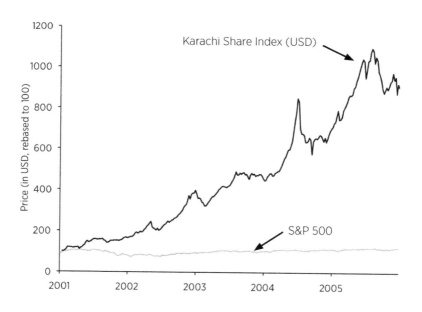

Chart 5.2. Performance of Karachi Share Index and S&P 500, September 2001-September 2006

A great example is Pakistan. In the decade following 11 September 2001, Pakistan made the headlines for violence, terrorism, floods, and a string of political and economic crises. The temptation, of course, would be to think that Pakistan was an awful place to put your money and to write it off as uninvestable. Yet this would have been a mistake: the country has a young population eager to get on and some excellent businesses, many of which were selling on two or three times earnings with double-digit yields. While the S&P 500 went up just 19% in the five years after the September 2001 attacks, the Karachi Share Index went up 854% in dollar terms, as shown in Chart 5.2.

It is not enough to just start out flexibly, you have to *stay* flexible as well. If you find a sound investment and it starts to work, you will find the market can be quite quick to cotton on, and the undervaluation disappears. Hence, today's stock market dogs and stars are not the same as those of five years ago, and will not be the same five years hence. Like a nomad, the value investor has to keep moving on to new pastures; turning to new bargains and selling out of yesterday's bargains when they become expensive.

Flexibility is the natural consequence of a disciplined approach to absolute value. Absolute value will kick you out of overvalued shares and popular strategies, sending you to look elsewhere.

True quality really is worth paying (a bit more) for

An especially important aspect of flexibility is the ability to identify and analyse high quality businesses. By quality, I mean a business with a long track record of high returns, a strong and sustainable competitive position, sensible management and reasonable prospects for growth. These are the sorts of companies that Warren Buffett and Charlie Munger are usually associated with and an obvious example would be a share like Coca-Cola.

If an investor had bought Coke shares in 1972, he would have paid a whopping 46x earnings. Nevertheless, the power of compound growth and sensible capital allocation delivered returns of 16% p.a. over the subsequent 25 years. While really great businesses like this are incredibly rare, they are worth paying significantly more for than mediocre or poor businesses. Chart 5.3 shows the total return of Coca-Cola from 1972 to the present day.

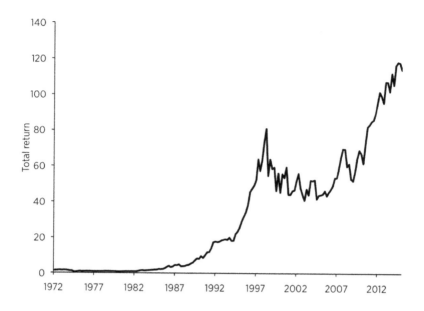

Chart 5.3. Coca-Cola, 1972-2015

There is no shortage of evidence supporting the case for investing in quality companies. For example, many studies have found low beta shares tend to outperform.[30] 'Low beta' means that the share is less volatile than average shares, reflecting factors such as operational stability and strong finances. Indeed, as we have already seen in Chapter 3, there are myriad studies demonstrating a strong link between financial strength (such as low debt and strong cash generation) and

---

30. See for example: Haugen, R. A., *The Inefficient Stock market: What Pays Off and Why* (Prentice Hall, 2001); Baker, M., Bradley, B. and Wurgler, J., 'Benchmarks as Limits to Arbitrage: Understanding the Low-Volatility Anomaly' *Financial Analysts Journal* 67:1 (2011); Hsu, J., Kudoh, H. and Yamada, T., 'When Sell-Side Analysts Meet High-Volatility Stocks: An Alternative Explanation for the Low Volatility Puzzle' *Journal of Investment Management* 11:2 (2013), pp. 28-46.

subsequent performance. Other studies have found outperformance among shares with consistently high levels of profitability.[31]

One area that has attracted a lot of interest in recent years is Joel Greenblatt's Magic Formula.[32] The Magic Formula ranks businesses in order of returns (with the highest returns at the top), and in order of valuation (lowest EV/EBIT at the top). You then add the rankings up and buy those with the lowest aggregate score.

The idea is to spot the most profitable businesses on low valuations, thereby combining quality and value. Back-tests of the Magic Formula and similar approaches combining low valuation and high profitability have shown very impressive outperformance, typically in the region of 5% to 20% annually.[33] In addition, the combination of valuation and profitability produces portfolios with lower volatility than either the market or pure low valuation strategies.

As well as the evidence in support of quality investing, there are two broad reasons why value investors should be willing to pay more for quality businesses.

The first is that growth within a strong franchise can be very valuable. The Coca-Cola example above is a good illustration of this. Even modest compound growth rates can be enormously valuable when the returns on capital are high.

---

31. Joyce, C. and Mayer, K., 'Profits for the Long Run: Affirming the Case for Quality', GMO LLC, GMO White Paper (June 2012).

32. Greenblatt, J. and Tobias, A., *The Little Book That Beats the Market* (New York: John Wiley & Sons, 2005).

33. See for example: Greenblatt, J. and Tobias, A. *The Little Book That Beats the Market* (New York: John Wiley & Sons, 2005) (US all caps and US large caps); Goldstein, M. L., Cho, B. J., Price N. and Yang, S., 'A Value Horse Race, Updating Our Failure Models', The Focus Portfolio (Empirical Research Partners LLC, February 2006), (Low EV/EBIT and high RoCE in the US); Montier, J. and Lancetti, S., 'The Little Note That Beats the Markets', Dresdner Kleinwort Wasserstein Global Equity Strategy (March 2006), (Low EV/EBIT and high RoCE in US, UK, Europe and Japan); Draaisma, T., Carr, R., Secker, G., Ng, E. and Swing C., 'European Strategy: What the Magic Formula Advocates Today' (Morgan Stanley Equity Research Europe, August 2007), (Low EV/EBITDA and high RoCE in Europe).

Secondly, quality businesses are more resilient during downturns. Strong balance sheets, strong market positions and the cushion of high profitability make them more able to weather the inevitable cycles. It is easy to under-appreciate how valuable this resilience can be. During a bad spell, weak businesses are more likely to run into financial or operational difficulties, forcing them to do things that destroy value, such as selling assets at fire-sale prices, raising equity or damaging their position through underinvestment. By contrast, quality businesses are less likely to suffer as deeply. Often they can exploit downturns by taking market share, improving the business or buying back shares cheaply. All this can make for a far more attractive long-term investment.

Having said all of this, no company can grow forever and no company is so good that you cannot overpay. The point is that there are times when you can get really good businesses for valuations that are not far above lower quality peers. Sometimes these are sporadic and rare examples, but sometimes it might be the case across the whole market. At these times it is best to pay the modest premium.

Hence, flexible value investing should not be viewed as just buying the very cheapest shares, but also employing specific screens and more generous valuation techniques to identify equally undervalued, high quality businesses.

5.4 Shareholder yield is more important than dividend yield

There is a tendency among value investors to overly obsess about dividend yields. While dividend yields are important and high yielding shares have generally outperformed, other valuation metrics – such as low multiples of book value, earnings, cash flows or sales – have proved more effective over the long run.[34]

---

34. See for example: O'Shaughnessy, J. P., *What Works on Wall Street: A Guide*

Why is this?

One of the problems among the highest yielding shares is that the dividend is often not sustainable and the share is priced as such to reflect a deteriorating outlook. Another problem is that a high dividend is not always the best use of capital. If the company's share is very cheap, it may be better to spend the money on share buybacks. If it has a lot of debt, it might be safer to pay this down. If it has great market opportunities, it might be better investing in the business. And if it is in a very cyclical industry, it is often prudent to build up a cash buffer in good times.

So companies clinging to a high dividend policy might not be doing the best thing for their shareholders in the long run. Companies that either raise equity (a costly process that dilutes existing shareholders) or debt in order to fund a dividend should almost always be avoided.

What does make dividends a good signal is that it indicates internal capital discipline. Capital discipline refers to how companies handle the money they have and the money they are making. Disciplined companies spend cautiously and frugally, preferring to pay down debt and reward shareholders, while undisciplined companies spend heavily on capex, M&A or frivolities (such as private jets and fancy new headquarters). As we saw in section 4.2, signs of capital discipline are a very powerful indicator of good things to come, while indiscipline is a very bad sign.

In order to capture the benefits of companies displaying capital discipline, it is better to use a wider measure than just dividends to get a more complete picture. This wider measure is called *shareholder yield*.[35]

Shareholder yield adds up the total spent on buybacks, dividends and debt pay-down and deducts money received from raising debt and equity. Most of these numbers can be found in the cash flow statement under 'Cash from financing activities' (although you'll need to swap

---

to the Best Performing Investment Strategies of All Time (New York: McGraw-Hill, 2007).

35. I can highly recommend Mebane Faber's short book, *Shareholder Yield: A Better Approach to Dividend Investing* (2013) for a good summary of the evidence and advantages behind shareholder yield investing.

the pluses and minuses around), and many stock screeners and data providers can provide these as well.

As Chart 5.4 shows (covering US shares from 1980 to 2010), investing in shares with the highest shareholder yield has delivered significantly higher returns than investing in shares with the highest dividend or buyback yields.

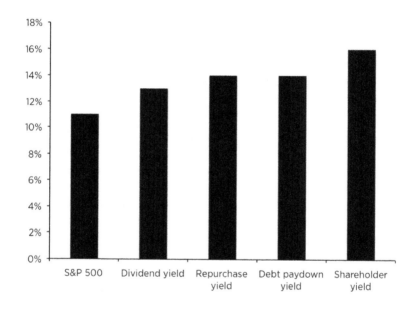

Chart 5.4. Investing in US shares with the highest shareholder yield

Source: Meb Faber Research[36]

In most cases, the total 'Cash from financing activities' number (with the plus or minus sign reversed) serves as a close approximation to shareholder yield. (In practice, the total cash from financing given in the cash flow statement may differ slightly from shareholder yield, as

36. Faber, M., 'A Near 50% Tax Rate on Dividends', Meb Faber Research [online] (October 2012), available online at: mebfaber.com/2012/10/09/a-50-tax-rate-on-dividends.

it often includes other inputs, such as foreign currency adjustments.) Ideally, you are looking to see a consistent record of capital discipline (in the form of negative cash from financing) over a number of years.

While finding the shareholder yield requires a bit more effort than the simple dividend metric, it has proven far more effective. Two recent studies have both found that shares with the highest shareholder yield typically outperform by around 4% per annum – about twice as much as the highest dividend shares.[37]

Another important feature of high shareholder yield is its record of low volatility and strong outperformance in downturns. If you feel markets are getting over-exuberant and may be due a correction, looking among the high yielders is a great place to start. Not only do they tend to provide better capital preservation, but (by paying out dividends or supporting their share prices through buybacks), they can provide the ammunition to move into the deeply undervalued bargains as they emerge.

One obvious problem for many investors is that they depend on income from their shares and a high shareholder yield portfolio is likely to have a lower yield than a conventional high dividend portfolio. The solution is still to use shareholder yield, but to supplement any shortfall in income with share sales.

While selling down shares may feel like depleting your reserves, it is really no different from taking a dividend. A dividend paid out *decreases* the underlying value remaining in the shares, while the company retaining the cash for debt paydown or buybacks will *increase* the underlying value per share. So selling some shares will leave you with fewer shares, but each share is now more valuable. There may be tax benefits as well, as capital gains taxes from asset sales may be lower than income taxes on dividends.

---

37. Bradshaw, M. T., Richardson, S. A. and Sloan, R. G., 'The Relation Between Corporate Financing Activities, Analysts' Forecasts and Stock Returns', *Journal of Accounting and Economics* 42:1-2 (2006), pp. 53-85; Gray, W. R. and Vogel, J., *Enhancing the Investment Performance of Yield-Based Strategies* (May, 2012), available at SSRN: ssrn.com/abstract=2051101.

5.5 Summary

- Always base buy and sell decisions on absolute valuations.

- Relying on relative valuations can be deceptive. However, comparing multiples with peers and historic levels can provide a useful sense-check.

- Value investing tends to work best among shares in the cheapest valuation deciles, so screening for these can be especially rewarding. But be prepared: these are often the least comfortable companies to invest in.

- Make sure you have the ability to act flexibly. Use a range of screens and valuation techniques to capture different value styles. In particular, be willing to pay a little more (both in screens and valuation) for high quality businesses (those with sustainably high returns, strong financials and sound prospects). Be willing to search broadly – across different markets and sectors – and to hold cash when there is a dearth of good opportunities.

- Do not obsess about dividend yields. Focus instead on shareholder yield as a truer and more valuable indicator of capital discipline.

PART III.
Strategy

CHAPTER 6.

Be Contrarian

6.1 Taking the dogs for a walk

"Many shall be restored that now are fallen and many shall fall that now are in honour."

From Horace's ***Ars Poetica***, quoted in
Security Analysis by Benjamin Graham[38]

I love tennis and I play quite a lot. But there are three months of the year when I hardly ever play. Those three months are June, July and August. Why? Because that's when everybody plays. Folk are on holiday, it's sunny and tournaments are on TV, inspiring Wimbledon wannabes. If you play at these times, not only do you have to queue for a court, but you then have to pay. Go at any other time of year and

---

38. Graham, B. and Dodd, D. L., *Security Analysis: The Classic 1951 Edition* (New York: McGraw-Hill, 2005).

the courts are empty, you can choose whatever court you want and play for as long as you want, the weather's cooler and fresher, and it's free.

That's one of the characteristics of people: they act in herds. Whether playing tennis, drinking a particular brand of beer, listening to a certain band, or choosing where to invest, people want to be part of the crowd. Often being part of the crowd makes sense and it feels easier. But equally often there are times when thinking for yourself and going against the grain has big advantages. It is a willingness to behave in a genuinely different way – often completely opposite to the majority – that defines a contrarian.

Contrarian investing involves acting in a way that is at odds with what most other investors are doing. This typically means buying into the most hated shares, industries and economies that others are throwing away, and shunning the most favoured. Contrarian investing may sound foolhardy and it is never comfortable, but it is one of those situations where going against the crowd has proved incredibly successful.

The above quote from Horace's *Ars Poetica* was chosen by Benjamin Graham as the opening line to *Security Analysis*. The fact that Graham – the godfather of value investing – chose this line above all others illustrates how central the contrarian approach is.

Since Graham, the contrarian mindset has been a defining feature among leading value investors. Warren Buffett famously advised, "Be fearful when others are greedy and greedy when others are fearful." But no one more lucidly epitomised the contrarian style than Sir John Templeton. For nearly 70 years Templeton scoured the world for neglected and unfavoured shares, in the process making billions for himself and his clients. His belief was always that, "To buy when others are despondently selling and to sell when others are avidly buying requires the greatest fortitude and pays the greatest ultimate rewards."

The importance of being different

One of my favourite market anecdotes is of an old widow, who, it turned out, had built up a sizable fortune from some very modest investing in US shares. People began asking what her secret was. It transpired she had simply been buying the cheapest shares she could find, just like she did with her groceries. Her idea of cheapness was that a share costing 20 cents was cheaper than one costing 50 cents!

In fact, studies later showed that this is one of the ultimate contrarian strategies. Because US shares are generally priced within a range of $10 to $50 and are split to keep them there, this naive approach was turning up only the most beaten up and neglected shares in the market. It goes to show that it's not about doing something clever that counts, but doing something different.

Unfortunately, most investors do not enjoy such good fortune. Active investing is a costly process, both in terms of time and money. After these costs are taken into account, the simple laws of arithmetic mean that the average active investor will lag a typical low-cost tracker fund by a meaningful margin. Indeed, the evidence has borne this out, with about 75% to 90% of professional actively managed funds underperforming their benchmark index over periods of five years or more, and the average individual investor faring even worse.

The only way to have a chance of recouping those extra costs is to invest in a way that is *extremely* different and to keep doing so. If you end up thinking like the market and holding a portfolio which is similar in composition to the wider market, you are wasting time and money. Investors unwilling to accept this should not even begin down the path of active management, as it will become increasingly evident that they are sacrificing more than they can gain.

It is no accident that all the great investors have been contrarians – they simply have to be. It is their very willingness to act independently and differently that enables them to achieve extraordinary results. Unsurprisingly, recent studies of institutional investors have shown this to be the case, with superior performance found among portfolios with the highest active share (active share measures the amount of differentiation between the portfolio's composition and a comparable index).[39]

---

39. Cremers, K. J. M. and Petajisto, A., 'How Active is Your Fund Manager? A New Measure that Predicts Performance', *Review of Financial Studies* 22:9 (2009), pp. 3329-3365; Petajisto, A., 'Active Share and Mutual Fund Performance' *Financial Analysts Journal* 69:4 (2013), pp. 73-93.

Unfortunately, examples of real differentiation amongst professional investors are incredibly rare. Many professional managers are doomed from the start, with so many restrictions and risk controls that it is simply impossible for them to be sufficiently different.

What's more, all managers face enormous industry-wide pressures to *index-hug*. Professional investors are constantly benchmarked against their peers, often over periods of as little as a few months. Those with the weakest short-term performance get fired. So the incentive is to try and stick as close as possible to the middle of the pack, because taking any sort of really differentiated approach will risk losing their clients and their jobs. Jim Melcher described the modern investment profession as, "Like a flock of sheep with wolves circling them. They band closer and closer together. You want to be somewhere in the middle of that flock."[40]

The herd-like way in which most asset managers now allocate the world's capital allows enormous and ultimately destructive imbalances to build up, leading to the painful booms and busts we regularly see on main street. While in many ways this is a tragedy, it also presents an opportunity. The potential rewards for the few who are willing and able to adopt a contrarian approach have, if anything, increased.

6.2 Empirical support for contrarian investing

The evidence supporting contrarian investment strategies is plentiful. Moreover, these studies are robust: covering many different markets over long time periods, they demonstrate that contrarian approaches work across different economic and political environments.

It is vital to appreciate the weight of the evidence, as well as to understand its implications. Contrarian investing is not instinctive. It

40. Quoted in: Authers, J., Book Extract: *The Fearful Rise of Markets*, *Financial Times Magazine* (May 2010).

requires nerves of steel and involves taking a leap of faith. You have to really believe in it before you can actually do it.

In this section I will summarise the results of a number of studies into contrarian investing.

'Does the Stock market Overreact?'[41]

Back-testing US shares from 1926 to 1982, Werner De Bondt and Richard Thaler found that constructing a portfolio of the shares with the *worst* three-year performance went on to outperform the market by 19.6% on average over the following three years. Meanwhile, the top performers of the past three years actually went on to underperform. The same held true for the worst five-year performers, which subsequently outperformed by 32% over the next five years, while the past five-year winners went on to disappoint.

While the researchers found that the outperformance of these 'loser' portfolios continued for five or six years, outperformance tended to be most significant in years two and three.

The authors explained their findings in terms of investor overreaction, whereby shares that have enjoyed a run of good results tend to become overvalued while those producing bad results eventually become undervalued. In practice, company performance tends to mean-revert.

A 50-year back-test of US shares by James P. O'Shaughnessy[42] affirmed De Bondt & Thaler's findings. He found that the decile of US shares with the worst prior five-year price performance went on to produce average outperformance of 4.2% over the next year, while those with the best prior performance lagged by nearly 6%.

---

41. De Bondt, W. F. M. and Thaler, R., 'Does the Stock market Overreact?', *Journal of Finance* 40:3 (1985), pp. 793-805.
42. O'Shaughnessy, J. P., *What Works on Wall Street: A Guide to the Best Performing Investment Strategies of All Time* (New York: McGraw-Hill, 2007).

'Mean Reversion in Stock Prices'[43]

James Poterba and Lawrence Summers found long-term mean reversion of share performance across the world. Their study covered 18 major stock markets from 1926/57 to 1985/6, including European, Asian and emerging economies. They found that share returns consistently mean revert over holding periods of two to eight years, with low investment returns preceding high returns and vice versa.

'Contrarian Investment, Extrapolation and Risk'[44]

One of the most important studies on the topic has suggested that value approaches are in fact just capturing the underperformance/ overreaction effect.

In their paper, Lakonishok, Shleifer and Vishny (LSV) found that combining a low valuation with low historic five-year sales growth led to significant outperformance amongst US shares. At the extreme, they found portfolios composed of the cheapest decile of shares (on measures such as low P/E, P/CF or low P/B) and with the *lowest* prior five-year sales growth, went on to outperform by over 100% cumulatively over the next five years. It is also stunning how results get gradually worse as shares get more expensive or have grown faster.

LSV's findings have since been affirmed and updated by the Brandes Institute. Brandes found similar results to LSV's original study across 23 global markets and using longer test periods.[45]

In effect, the approach involves buying not only cheap shares but also those that are out of favour. Combining a value and contrarian strategy has the advantage of avoiding seemingly cheap shares that are only cheap because their earnings or assets are at peak levels. Instead, you

43. Poterba, J. and Summers, L. H., 'Mean Reversion in Stock Prices: Evidence and Implications', *Journal of Financial Economics* 22 (1988), pp 27-59.

44. Lakonishok, J., Shleifer, A. and Vishny, R. W., 'Contrarian Investment, Extrapolation, and Risk', *The Journal of Finance* 49:5 (1994), pp. 1541-1578.

45. 'Value Versus Glamour: A Global Phenomenon' (The Brandes Institute, November 2012), available online at www.brandes.com/institute/research.

not only get a low valuation multiple, but it is a low multiple of already distressed earnings or asset values.

'Expectations and the Cross-Section of Stock Returns'[46]

La Porta's study found that the top decile of shares rated as having the best earnings growth prospects by professional analysts went on to return a full 21% per year *less* than the most hated decile of shares that were expected to shrink or stagnate. The author explained the findings in terms of overly optimistic forecasts for the glamour shares and overly pessimistic ones for the dogs. These forecasting errors usually took several years to correct.

In a study for his book, *Contrarian Investment Strategies*, David Dreman made a similar finding.[47] He examined the subsequent performance of the top picks from professional investor surveys between 1929 and 1993. He found that only 25% of the time did the experts' 'best' shares outperform the S&P 500 over the next year. This is clearly far worse than what could be achieved even from just picking shares at random.

'Falling Knives Around the World'[48]

In this study, the Brandes Institute examined the subsequent performance of shares that had fallen more than 60% in the previous year. These shares are often referred to as *falling knives*.

The study covered both US and international shares from 1980 to 2003. It found that a strategy of investing in falling knives delivered outperformance of around 6% per year over a three-year holding period.

---

46. La Porta, R., 'Expectations and the Cross-Section of Stock Returns' *The Journal of Finance* 51:5 (1996), pp. 1715-1742.

47. Dreman, D., *Contrarian Investment Strategies: The Next Generation* (New York: Simon & Schuster, 1998), pp. 84-87.

48. 'Falling Knives Around the World' (The Brandes Institute, August 2004), available online at www.brandes.com/institute/research.

While that may seem impressive, Brandes found that investing in the quartile of falling knives with the lowest enterprise value-to-sales ratios (a measure that rewards both low valuation and low levels of debt) returned around 12% per year outperformance.

In addition, however, the authors make two very important points. Firstly, failure rates can be high among these shares, with the average pulled up by a minority of very big winners. And secondly, long holding periods are essential – almost all the outperformance comes in years two and three.

Distress shares

Related to this are a wide array of other studies of severely distressed shares, including those with negative shareholders equity and loss-making companies with negative P/Es. While not cheap on some conventional measures, baskets of these highly distressed shares have been shown to deliver impressive subsequent outperformance in a variety of studies from around the world.[49]

When overreaction runs out of steam[50]

The above studies show how successful buying out-of-favour shares can be. However, it is also important to understand how the underperformance corrects.

It has been found that cheap and out-of-favour shares typically do a lot better around announcements of earnings or other events. When those announcements are positive surprises, the unpopular shares tend to go up a lot. However, even when those announcements are negative,

---

49. For example see: Fama, E. and French, K. R., 'The Cross-Section of Expected Stock Returns', *Journal of Finance* 47:2 (1992), pp. 427-465; Jaffe, J., Keim, D. B. and Westerfield, R., 'Earnings Yields, Market Values, and Stock Returns', *Journal of Finance* 44:1 (1989), pp. 135-148; Chan, L. K. C., Hamao, Y. and Lakonishok, J., 'Fundamentals and Stock Returns in Japan', *Journal of Finance* 46:5 (1991), pp. 1739-1764.
50. Dreman, D., *Contrarian Investment Strategies: The Next Generation* (New York: Simon & Schuster, 1998); La Porta, R., 'Expectations and the Cross-Section of Stock Returns', *The Journal of Finance* 51:5 (1996), pp. 1715-1742.

they don't tend to go down much. By contrast, when the stock market darlings deliver yet more good news, the shares barely budge, but when they under-deliver they take a big knock.

This gives us some idea of how contrarian investing works. When pessimism or optimism gets driven to extremes, sooner or later it reaches a point where it simply cannot go any further. It is all but impossible to beat expectations for eternal perfection, just as it is easy to beat expectations for unremitting disaster. From such points, valuations must normally correct.

Note that this process is gradual. Dreman's research suggests dogs are still benefiting from positive news more than negative news as much as five years later. It normally takes a long time for an unloved share to regain favour, or for the market to fall out of love with a star.

The relationship between value investing and contrarian investing

The key takeaway from this section is how closely related successful value investing is with contrarian investing. Most shares on cheap valuations will have already suffered a run of poor performance and will have become either neglected or actively disliked. And the most undervalued shares tend to be the ones with the worst prior performance, as that is what causes the market to underestimate their potential.

The conclusion is that value investors need to be willing to buy shares that are not just cheap, but also unpopular and often with obvious problems. In fact, just buying lowly valued shares that have performed well (either share price or sales growth) does not work. These tend to be shares that are near their cyclical peaks and everyone can see they are headed for trouble (hence the low multiples). So in these cases the extrapolation and mean reversion effects do not help.

In addition, the research also demonstrates the importance of patience. It generally requires holding periods of three to five years to reap the rewards.

6.3 Why does contrarianism work?

The overreaction hypothesis

As we have seen, there is overwhelming evidence supporting contrarian investing. But how and why does it happen? The most common explanation is investor overreaction. That is, investors overreact to a string of positive news events or positive opinions, eventually leading to a share becoming overvalued. Conversely, they also overreact to a string of negative news events or unfavourable opinions, eventually leading to a share becoming undervalued. Thus, after a few years, good news shares end up overvalued and bad news shares undervalued.

Having explained the process, it is now time to understand why investors overreact.

Investor psychology

Investing is a psychological activity. Decisions are made based on how our minds process and respond to information. Unfortunately, the human mind does not always process information perfectly and this can lead to misjudgments.

Psychologists call the most common types of misjudgments behavioural biases. These biases are instinctive. In investing, they can cause many investors to collectively make the same misjudgment at the same time, leading to a significant undervaluation or overvaluation. Contrarian investing exploits several of the most prevalent biases, which are discussed below.

Over-extrapolation

Looking for patterns is one of the most powerful instincts we have. This is because in evolutionary terms humans had to learn very quickly in a hostile environment. The result is that investors will often extrapolate trends as a matter of course, even where there is no good reason to do so. Hence, investors overpay for companies with strong recent performance in the expectation that it will continue, while shunning anything that does poorly, in the belief that things must carry on getting worse.

While the tendency is to put a lot of faith in historic patterns and identify reasons for them continuing, in the harsh reality of a highly competitive, adaptive and unpredictable world, most trends – both positive and negative – eventually revert to more normal levels, or reverse.

Recency bias

People generally put too much emphasis on recent events that are fresh in the memory, rather than considering longer-term trends. Think of all the times when you've felt like something was the most important thing happening and a few months later you can barely remember it. Well, that is recency bias.

Recency bias means that investors often overreact to recent news. If the recent news is good they get overexcited and overpay. If recent news is bad they get overly depressed and sell cheaply.

A good example is Warren Buffett's famous purchase of Coca-Cola in 1988. At the time, investors were obsessing about the weak recent sales growth and the flop that was 'New Coke' a few years earlier. Meanwhile, they ignored the longer-term trends of growing consumption, brand-building and successful international expansion that had been going on for decades. Identifying the mismatch between short-term difficulties and sound long-term prospects is at the heart of successful contrarian investing.

Association

Vanity is a powerful thing. People care about how they are perceived. Decisions such as the clothes we wear, the car we drive, how we talk or where we live are based on how we want to be perceived. Investors often choose shares in the same way. Hence they overpay for what is seen as successful or fashionable, for the same reasons that shoppers pay up for designer labels. By contrast, investors will shun apparently weak or troubled companies because they feel it somehow reflects on themselves.

Institutional factors

Institutional investors dominate modern stock markets, typically accounting for over 80% of volumes. These institutions generally take a 'buy-high, sell-low' approach to investing, for a number of reasons.

Firstly, investment decisions are usually made by committees rather than individuals. This makes it hard to get approval for anything which has problems or faces uncertainty. Then there is the issue of presenting to clients and senior management. It is always easier to present portfolios full of well-known and successful glamour shares, rather than troubled or neglected businesses that are either making headlines for the wrong reasons, or not making headlines at all. The result is that whatever is flavour-of-the-month gets bought up, and whatever looks ugly gets booted out, almost regardless of value.

Then there are the institutional pressures to chase whatever is going up and in vogue (index trackers do this too). A share's size and liquidity matters to institutions, so they will buy something after it has gone up (when it is bigger and more liquid) and sell it after it has gone down (and is considered to be too small).

By behaving in this herd-like way, the overall effect of institutional behaviour is often to exacerbate the overvaluation and undervaluation of shares. Contrarian investors can profit by taking the opposite position to these large institutions and exploiting the opportunities they have created.

Supply and demand

The most basic lesson of economics is that the price of something is determined by supply and demand. When demand is high and supply is low, the price will be high. When demand is subdued and supply is plentiful, the price will be low.

When a share or market has done well and its prospects look good, demand will be at its peak and there will be few sellers. But once everyone likes it, there is no new demand left to drive the price any higher. All that can happen from here is that some will fall out of love with it and the price will get lower.

Once again, the converse is also true: a share or market that everyone hates will have been sold down by everyone who is going to sell, pushing supply to its peak while demand hits rock bottom. From this point, any improvement in popularity and the price can only go up. Hence, Sir John Templeton's famous maxim, "The time of maximum pessimism is the best time to buy and the time of maximum optimism is the best time to sell."

Capital and hubris cycles at the corporate level

When companies, industries or countries get into trouble, they generally do something about it. Troubled companies might improve their products, cut costs, buy back shares or bring in new management. Troubled industries will normally consolidate or take out capacity, while troubled economies will see their currencies weaken and may push through reforms.

By contrast, successful businesses tend to do the opposite. They become complacent and often blow their burgeoning profits on vanity projects or over-expansion.

Moreover, past success can actually inspire disaster. High growth or profitability encourages competitors to copy the incumbent and also attracts new entrants. Often governments attack successful businesses too (e.g. through taxes or anti-trust laws). All these new pressures are likely to bring down profitability and growth over time. There is even evidence that technological advances and globalisation are making the success curse even worse, suggesting that good companies lose their edge even more quickly than in the past.[51]

---

51. Wiggins, R. R. and Ruefli, T. W., 'Schumpeter's Ghost: Is Hypercompetition Making the Best of Times Shorter?', *Strategic Management Journal* 26:10 (2005), pp. 887-911.

6.4 Contrarianism as protection

As well as offering a lot of upside, a contrarian outlook can offer protection against some of the most common errors in investing.

One of the most dangerous mistakes is buying into a share near a cyclical peak. Often shares can appear deceptively cheap in boom times. As well as boosting earnings, cyclical booms and speculative bubbles encourage companies to overstretch themselves financially. When the inevitable bust comes, the combination of collapsing earnings and spiralling liabilities can obliterate shareholder wealth.

Some banks and house-builders were on low P/E multiples in 2007, but as the real estate bubble burst, many of these shares lost over 90% of their value and some were driven to bankruptcy. This is by no means unusual. For example, in mid-2007 RBS might have looked cheap to some investors, with a P/E of less than 9 and a 4.5% dividend yield. However, the bank's business model was heavily dependent on the credit cycle, meaning these results were unsustainable. As the cycle reversed, RBS shareholders lost over 95%, as shown in Chart 6.1.

Most value investors don't want to get into the mug's game of making big economic predictions. However, avoiding bubbles is clearly important. This is where a contrarian approach really helps. By focusing on companies in depressed sectors, that have not seen rapid sales growth, asset growth or booming valuations, it is highly unlikely that you will buy into an unsustainable boom.

Now and again, managements make disastrous errors of judgment, which leads to them overreaching themselves through M&A, over-expansion, or diversification. Management folly is most commonly down to hubris, and hubris occurs when management have something to be hubristic about – that is to say after the company has been performing well.

When it comes to lowly contrarian shares, it seems bad performance begets good management. After a poor run, management tend to be humble, with their focus firmly on controlling costs and turning around existing operations rather than chasing some delusion of grandeur. Once all the problems are laid out, management have things

to focus on. Clear problems bring out ingenuity and a roadmap back
to better times.

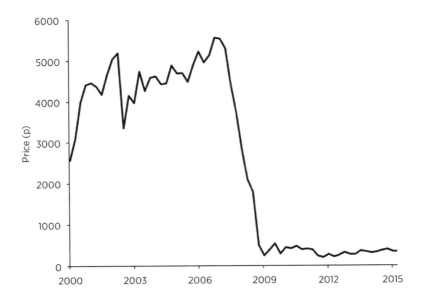

Chart 6.1. RBS share price, March 2000-March 2015

In addition, one of the most common problems investors have is being
overly optimistic and failing to see potential problems before they
happen. This leads them to overpay for shares based on unrealistic
expectations. Fortunately this is not a problem many contrarians
share. When a share has been doing badly for a prolonged period,
anyone reviewing it is more likely to be overly pessimistic. By then,
the problems and investment risks are normally out in the open and
widely understood.

Being overly pessimistic is fine. At best, you get an even better bargain
than you realise and at worst you miss out on the odd opportunity (not
to worry, you can always find another). By contrast, over-optimism is
disastrous: the money is lost for good, there is an opportunity cost in

that a better investment is forgone, and the exercise has been a waste of time. This is why successful investors from Warren Buffett to Seth Klarman place so much emphasis on not losing money.

By avoiding over-optimism, sidestepping booms and busts, and skipping the worst management excesses, contrarian approaches provide excellent downside protection.

6.5 Crisis investing

Contrarians love a crisis

Crises regularly engulf markets, sectors or even the whole world. Pretty much any share anywhere gets caught up in a crisis every few years. Even defensive shares in seemingly safe countries suffer crises. For example, the US Healthcare sector sold-off heavily in 2009/10 on fears over ObamaCare. As those fears subsided, it was possible to make five or ten times your money in many of the companies in this sector.

As David Dreman observes, "A market crisis presents an outstanding opportunity, because it lets loose overreaction at its wildest."[52] During a crisis investors become hypnotised by the collapsing prices, flow of awful news and predictions of extreme disaster. In doing so, they lose focus on intrinsic value, leaving opportunities wide open for those who can remain level-headed. Really successful value investors typically make most of their money by investing into crises.

It is important to appreciate that investment returns are not even. A successful investor's record will contain years when they were down 25% and other years when they were up 100%, rather than a smooth pattern of steady returns year on year.

---

52. Dreman, D., *Contrarian Investment Strategies: The Next Generation* (New York: Simon & Schuster, 1998), pp. 261.

A common pattern among great investors is to lag in late-stage bull-markets as highly speculative shares get driven up and up, then hold up well in the subsequent sell-off, and then, having bought the most beaten up names, make a fortune in the recovery. The point is that big money is made from making those contrarian calls now and again, having the courage to really back them and then hanging on till that view is proved right.

Of course, actually investing into a crisis is remarkably difficult. The first thing to contend with is media doom and gloom. Predictions of Armageddon and impending collapse attract viewers and sell newspapers, so the media will go completely overboard. Long lines of 'experts' are drafted in to make lurid predictions of imminent disaster. Soon the public are hooked on their daily dose of misery. Phrases such as "It'll never be the same again" and "It can only get worse" get bandied about. Panic becomes the widespread default position.

A widely underappreciated fact is that herd behaviour is far greater in bear markets than bull markets. In happy or relaxed times, people are willing to do their own thing to some extent. But in a time of real crisis, panic or confusion, there is an overwhelming instinct to shun individualism for the safety of the herd. The image that comes to mind is of a panicking crowd, dropping everything and just running for the exits. The overriding urge is to get away and think later. With so much self-reinforcing hyperbole and herd behaviour, it is no wonder market crises create so many undervalued opportunities.

Needless to say, when a crisis has hit a market or sector, you normally don't want to be selling, but buying.

In his book on contrarian investing[53], David Dreman examined the 11 largest market crises between World War II and 1990. Some of these were caused by economic problems, others by geopolitical events (e.g. the Cuban Missile Crisis, the Kennedy assassination and the Gulf War) and others for no obvious reason (e.g. the 1987 crash). He found that in the two years after a crisis, returns averaged 38%. This is a spectacular result. While it is impossible to pick the bottom, even buying a good bit too early would still have delivered stellar results. By

---

53. Dreman, D., *Contrarian Investment Strategies: The Next Generation* (New York: Simon & Schuster, 1998), pp.263.

contrast, selling in the panics would have sacrificed many incredible opportunities.

Thinking back to 2008-2009

It is important to understand that buying into a deep crisis will invariably mean acting alone. You cannot expect support from colleagues, peers or the financial pages. Before the financial crisis I had been fortunate to move most of my funds into cash and shares which held up well (most actually went up during 2008). From about November 2008, I began buying aggressively into the most obvious bargains. In many cases these were companies trading at a fraction of their net cash value – something that is hard to believe was possible now. By early March 2009, I had invested everything I had and taken on a sizable personal debt as well.

Most of what I had bought was continuing to fall. What I remember most vividly from the time was reading the Weekend Edition of the *Financial Times* – something I did every Saturday. Every single week throughout the crisis, there was always someone bullish, giving reasons why things were about to turn. Then one weekend in late March, across the whole paper, there was not one positive comment left. The news flow could not get worse; everyone believed markets were going lower and that meant everyone who was going to sell had sold. Chart 6.2 shows the FTSE 100 at this time.

And that was how the biggest stock market crisis of modern times ended, giving way to a phenomenal bull market. Over the subsequent four years, the capital gains taxes I paid on the shares I bought during this period exceeded the total amount I had invested.

It later transpired that in the weeks surrounding the bottom, the market had been dominated not by the usual big institutions, but by low volumes of small, individual buyers. The 'sophisticated' investors were nowhere in sight. The best contrarians are always individuals.

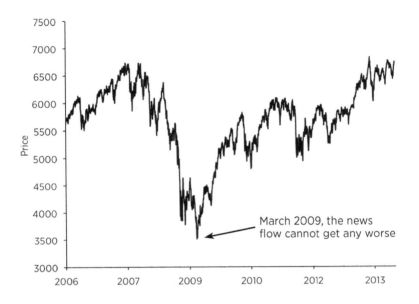

Chart 6.2. FTSE 100, 2006-2013

The mechanics of crisis investing

Crisis investing is really just a form of extreme value investing. It requires a consistent focus on long-term fundamental value to take advantage of widespread overreaction to negative news-flow.

When you look at them this way, crises start to look a lot more attractive than bull markets. A business' true worth depends on its cash flows over its lifetime. When the price is high the cash flow yield is low; when the price falls, the cash flow yield goes higher.

So if prices double in a bull market, the cash flow and dividend yields halve. Are you now better off? Nope: not unless you're selling. Bull markets are actually very bad news for investors who are net savers, because it costs more to get the same cash flows as before. Meanwhile, deep crises are good, because you are getting a bigger cash flow yield than before. A crisis is like your bank offering to double the interest rate on your savings account.

In practice, major crises rarely have a significant impact on long-term values. For example, Research Affiliates[54] looked at the ten biggest US bear markets over the past century and found that while the average share fell 46% in real terms, the average real dividend fell just 2.7%. In a crisis, you get a lot more bang for your buck.

'Investor Sentiment and the Cross-Section of Stock Returns'[55]

Completed in 2000 and back testing data on US shares from 1935 to 2000, Baker and Wurgler's work represents one of the most important leaps in our understanding of markets and is a truly valuable treasure for contrarian investors. What the study did that makes it so striking was to examine how stock market sentiment influences subsequent returns.

The pair were able to quantify sentiment by looking at a variety of factors such as the number of IPOs, share turnover and the premium on dividend-paying shares. Fortunately for investors, in real life it should be fairly clear when sentiment is particularly high or low.

What the authors discovered was striking – several factors which have little aggregate relevance actually reveal themselves to be powerful predictors of future returns once market sentiment is considered. Investor sentiment affects what factors work.

They found that when sentiment was low:

- Small shares sharply outperformed larger shares. Indeed, the long-term superior returns of small shares can be explained by their sharp recoveries from bear markets, not during more normal upbeat periods.

---

54. Arnott, R., 'Institutionalizing Courage', *Research Affiliates Newsletter* (May 2012).
55. Baker, M. and Wurgler, J., 'Investor Sentiment and the Cross-section of stock returns', *The Journal of Finance* 61:4 (2006), pp. 1645-1680.

- Very young shares (recent IPOs) outperform older, more established companies.

- Shares with very high sales growth also outperform.

- Shares displaying high volatility outperform more stable shares.

- Unprofitable shares with no earnings outperform profitable shares.

- Shares which pay no dividend outperform those that do.

- Shares showing signs of distress (such as shares with very low price-to-book ratios) also went on to beat others.

But when sentiment is high, these factors completely reverse – i.e. it is generally better to buy big, established, stable and profitable businesses paying dividends.

What the study really shows is that the sort of shares that triumph after market crises have a high degree of subjectivity in terms of valuation. This is because generally their businesses are highly changeable and they lack common factors (such as earnings or dividends) to value them by. In good times, investors and speculators are prone to see their good points and get over-optimistic, thereby overpaying – pinning a very high valuation on them. In bad times, investors see their bad sides and the risks that go with them, thereby abandoning them at very low levels in spite of their potential, in favour of more stable fare.

So what does all this mean?

It means that in the normal or good times, the contrarian can profit by being cautious and searching out sensible, stable shares at moderate valuations. But in times of fear, he should turn his sights on the stuff that feels most risky and speculative. It is buying stability when stability is under-appreciated, and buying volatility and risk when there is fear of instability. This is exactly what Warren Buffett meant when he advised investors to "Be greedy when others are fearful and fearful when others are greedy."

By inter-layering well-known metrics with market sentiment, the study represents a real leap in thinking. It provides both a charter and a road-map for true contrarians.

6.6 The trouble with contrarianism

Emotional discomfort

Contrarianism sounds great till you try it. In practice it is always a testing experience. For professional investors facing institutional pressures and constant scrutiny, those difficulties are redoubled. As a contrarian your opinions are different, so you constantly have to wrestle with widespread scepticism and challenge. When you are right, you are resented and do not have others to share in your successes. When you are wrong, you stand out like a sore thumb, and the sense of embarrassment can feel especially sharp.

By contrast, being part of the crowd and making consensus decisions feels easy, like swimming with the tide. When things are going well, everyone is congratulating each other. When things go badly, there is a sense of solidarity and that it was unavoidable because 'everyone got it wrong.' As John Maynard Keynes wrote, "Worldly wisdom teaches that it is better to fail conventionally than to succeed unconventionally."[56]

Nevertheless, it is important to remember that contrarianism is not for its own sake, and now and again the prevailing wisdom is right. So you need to have a sound, clear process sorted out before you start sticking your neck out. If your process is not sound it will fail anyway: it won't work just because it is contrarian, and if it works it will be because it is logical.

Long time horizons reward contrarian investors

As the evidence discussed in section 6.2 demonstrates, contrarian investment approaches tend to work effectively over long holding periods of two to eight years, with the best returns usually apparent in years two to five. Crucially, contrarian investing delivers generally poor results over holding periods of a year or less. Over short periods, the momentum effect is far more powerful. It takes much longer for really out of favour shares to turn their operations around and to regain confidence.

---

56. Keynes, J. M., *The General Theory of Employment, Interest and Money* (London: Macmillan & Co., 1936), Chapter 12.

One recent study on the subject was carried out by behavioural finance expert James Montier. It was aptly titled, *Just a Little Patience.*[57] Covering 1991 to 2006, the study consisted of a value strategy of buying the lowest P/E quintile of European shares and holding them. The outperformance in the first year averaged 3%, rising to 5% over two years, and 32% over five years. So the pick-up in outperformance during years three to five is 8% to 10% per annum. Moreover, as the holding period lengthens out, an increasingly large proportion of the shares become outperformers. Montier found similar results from buying a low price-to-book portfolio.

Very long holding periods have other advantages as well. In particular they cut down trading costs (such as spreads, commissions and market impact costs) which can often eat up several percent a year. Less trading can also lower tax bills.

All said and done, there are very clear benefits to value investors from extending time horizons. As Mr. Montier concludes, "Patience is the prerequisite for value investors."

Going against conventional wisdom is hard enough on its own. Unfortunately, the short-term momentum effect makes it harder still. When you buy an out-of-favour share, the chances are that it will get cheaper before things get better. Having stuck your neck out from the crowd and with your new share fresh in the mind, it may be just as likely to carry on falling as it is to turnaround.

Contrarian investors need to realise from the start that the wait is likely to be long and uncomfortable. This is the edge that prevents most investors from acting like contrarians and reaping the rewards. Most cannot accept the short-term pain, even where they appreciate the long-term opportunity.

In order to accept the short-term discomfort, it is necessary to adopt the right attitude towards your investments. As a minimum, you need a relaxed outlook and long-term focus. Always assess results over periods of many years or decades, and never over shorter periods.

---

57. Montier, J., *Behavioural Investing: A Practitioner's Guide to Applying Behavioural Finance* (Chichester: John Wiley & Sons, 2007), pp. 375-386.

6.7 Summary

- The willingness and ability to act very differently is a prerequisite for successful investing. It has been the hallmark of all successful long-term investors.

- There is very strong evidence that investing in shares that have suffered a prolonged period of weak performance and/or which are widely disliked is a highly profitable strategy. By contrast, investing in current favourites after they have done well normally leads to disappointing results.

- There is a close relationship between contrarian investing and value investing. This is because the really beaten up shares tend to be where the most undervalued opportunities are to be found.

- Why so? Because most investors are drama queens. They consistently get overexcited about what they perceive to be the best opportunities and overly pessimistic about what they view as the worst. In so doing they create opportunities for the few who are more independent.

- A contrarian bent can mitigate important risks such as bubbles, management hubris and over-optimism.

- Contrarian investing is highly profitable because it is difficult to do in practice, due to psychological instincts and institutional pressures. Contrarian investing involves standing up to conventional wisdom and often being wrong, at least for a while. It is not only a lonely pursuit but a discomfiting one. Even the fantastic long-term financial rewards are not sufficient to tempt many.

- Contrarian investing works over long holding periods, typically lasting several years. It does not generally work over shorter periods. Investors and their clients need to appreciate this, adopt a relaxed and patient attitude, and focus only on the very long term.

CHAPTER 7.

Buying the Best Bargains

7.1 Go global

Bargains are not evenly distributed around the world. At any one time, some national stock markets will have plenty of undervalued shares, while others will have hardly any. Thus, it is helpful to have the flexibility to invest in as many markets as possible. This enables the investor to widen the opportunity set and buy the very best bargains, wherever they may be. A recent study by James Montier[58] demonstrated how large increases in the performance of simple value strategies can be achieved simply by widening the field from a regional universe to a global one.

Moreover, value investors should be aware that when national stock markets trade on very cheap multiples, they are usually excellent buying opportunities. For example, a series of studies by Michael Keppler[59]

---

58. Montier, J., *Value Investing: Tools and Techniques for Intelligent Investment* (John Wiley & Sons Ltd., 2009).
59. Keppler, M. A., 'Further Evidence on the Predictability of International Equity Returns: The Importance of Cash Flow in Country Selection', *The*

found that the cheapest quartile of global stock markets (based on price-to-cash flow or dividend yield) outperformed the global index by nearly 7% a year.

More recently, the cyclically adjusted P/E (also called the CAPE or Shiller P/E) has been attracting a lot of attention. The CAPE measures a stock market's value divided by its average, inflation-adjusted earnings over the past ten years. By using ten-year average earnings, it smoothes out cyclical effects.

A large body of evidence has found the CAPE to be one of the few reliable predictors of future stock market returns, particularly over periods of three to five years.[60] Investing in low CAPE stock markets has tended to prove a very effective strategy, while investing in high CAPE stock markets has delivered very poor returns.

For example, Mebane Faber's global study[61] found that investing in markets when the CAPE was below 10 delivered a five-year average real return of over 17% per annum. By contrast, investing in markets with CAPEs above 50 gave average real returns of -6.4% – a truly awful result! Taken together, these studies show the incredible benefits of bargain-hunting in cheap and out-of-favour stock markets.

Table 7.1 and Chart 7.1 show the superior long-term returns from low-CAPE stock markets versus high-CAPE stock markets (1980-2011).[62]

Journal of Portfolio Management 18:1 (1991), pp. 48-53; Keppler, M. A., 'The Importance of Dividend Yields in Country Selection', *Journal of Portfolio Management* 17:2 (1991), pp. 24-29.

60. Faber, M. T., 'Global Value: Building Trading Models with the 10 Year CAPE', Cambria Quantitative Research, No. 5 (August 2012); Angelini, N., Bormetti, G., Marmi, S. and Nardini, F., 'Value Matters: Predictability of Stock Index Returns' (2012), available at SSRN: ssrn.com/abstract=2031406; Klement, J., 'Does the Shiller-PE work in Emerging Markets?', (2012), available at SSRN: ssrn.com/abstract=2088140.

61. Faber, M. T., 'Global Value: Building Trading Models with the 10 Year CAPE', Cambria Quantitative Research, No. 5 (August 2012).

62. Ibid.

Initial CAPE of stock market	Average one-year real return	Average three-year real return (per annum)	Average five-year real return (per annum)
<10	26%	17%	17%
10-15	23%	14%	12%
15-20	11%	11%	11%
20-25	4%	4%	6%
25-30	-1%	1%	3%
30-40	3%	-1%	-1%
40-50	-3%	-3%	0%
>50	-5%	-12%	-6%

Table 7.1. Superior long-term returns from low-CAPE stock markets

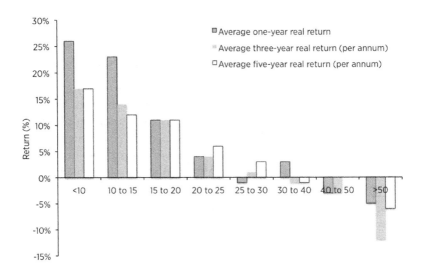

Chart 7.1. Superior long-term returns from low-CAPE stock markets

Thus, it is often worth devoting extra attention to national stock markets that appear very cheap on valuation measures such as CAPE. An in-depth search of those countries' shares may throw up many attractive opportunities.

While the benefits of investing globally are clear, investors should first familiarise themselves with the quirks of foreign stock markets. For example, there may be differences in how accounts are presented, different corporate governance standards and procedures, foreign ownership restrictions, and so on.

Value measures in emerging markets

One common question is whether value measures work as well in emerging markets as they have in developed countries. This is important as developing economies are becoming an increasingly significant part of many investment portfolios. At the same time, emerging countries are different in many ways to developed markets and most have been growing significantly faster, so one cannot just assume that the same rules apply.

The good news is that, so far, the evidence suggests that strategies of buying cheaply valued emerging market companies not only work, but work even better than comparable strategies in developed markets.[63]

Various explanations for this have been put forward. The first is that emerging markets are less efficient than developed markets. In other words, shares are less well covered so valuation anomalies are more likely to arise unnoticed. Another is that emerging economies tend to be more volatile, so shares tend to swing to greater extremes in terms of overvaluation and undervaluation. Hence value measures that identify

---

63. See for example: Adrian, S., Yang, S. and Sapp, W., 'The Emerging Markets: Valuation – The Secret Weapon' (Empirical Research Partners LLC, September 2009); Fama, E. F. and French, K. R., 'Value Versus Growth: The International Evidence', *Journal of Finance* 53:6 (1998), pp. 1975-1999; Kapur, A., Luk, P. and Samadhiya, R., 'Stock-picking – Minefields, Fertile Acres', Deutsche Bank AG/Hong Kong Global Markets Research (January 2011); 'Value vs. Glamour: Emerging Markets' (The Brandes Institute, April 2013), available online at www.brandes.com/institute/research.

distress or great pessimism – such as low P/S and low P/B – have proved especially effective in times of fear.

Interestingly, dividend yields have also proved consistently and highly effective. This may reflect typically weaker corporate governance in emerging countries. Hence companies paying money out are often preferable to those which retain it to invest at low returns or to be siphoned off.

What to do about foreign currency risks

Currency volatility can have meaningful effects on short-term returns. For example, if I buy a Japanese share and its price goes up 20% while the yen goes down 20%, the currency movement has undone all my upside. Equally, if both the yen and the share go up 20%, my return is doubled.

Unfortunately, most investors do not have strong views on currencies or the skill-set for making such forecasts. So a common question is, should I hedge currency risk? Currency hedging involves the use of derivatives to cancel out any changes in the value of foreign shares due to currency movements. Note that hedging involves consistently putting on new hedges for the duration of the investment: doing so intermittently with the aim of profiting from the hedging trades themselves is not hedging at all – it is speculating.

While currency hedging can seem an appealing way to remove an unwanted risk, investors are generally better off accepting the volatility. This is because, firstly, currency hedging is costly (as well as time consuming), and those costs will hurt long run returns. Moreover, over the long run, the positive (lucky) currency swings are likely to at least cancel out the negative (unlucky) ones, simply by the workings of chance.

To make matters worse, evidence shows that currency hedging actually *increases* volatility and *decreases* long-run returns![64] This is

---

64. Froot, K. A., 'Currency Hedging over Long Horizons National Bureau of Economic Research', NBER Working Paper No. 4355 (Cambridge, Mass.: NBER, May 1993).

because shares represent claims on real assets. In buying a real asset, you automatically hedge the currency. For example, if a central bank were to tighten interest rates, share prices are likely to fall, but the upward movement in the currency driven by the rate hike will offset the downward movement in the stock market. By hedging, you would forgo the currency appreciation while still suffering the stock market falls.

For global value investors, hedging may be especially counter-productive. Many value investments are likely to be made in weak economies, with cheap stock markets and weak currencies. As that economy will hopefully recover along with the share, a successful investment will often enjoy an extra currency kicker as well.

Indeed, a recent long-term study[65] found that stock market returns (in US dollars) were about *three* times higher in the countries that had suffered the worst currency depreciation compared to those with the strongest currencies. Currency falls often lead to low valuations, high returns and profitability (as the cost of capital goes up) and improved competitiveness (thanks to currency weakness and self-help). The conclusion is that you should not fear investing in an economy that has suffered from a weak currency.

7.2 Go small

The success of small caps

Historically, companies with smaller market caps have delivered higher returns for investors than those with the largest market caps. This is often called the *size effect*.

---

65. Dimson, E., Marsh, P., Staunton, M., Wilmot, J. and McGinnie, P., 'Credit Suisse Global Investment Returns Yearbook 2012', Credit Suisse Research (2012), pp. 17-27.

The size effect is demonstrated for the UK by Chart 7.2, showing the performance of the Numis Smaller Companies index against that of the FTSE 100 index for the period January 2000 to May 2015.

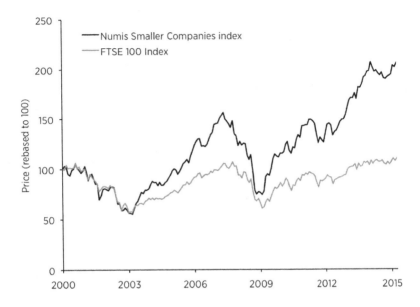

Chart 7.2. Numis Smaller Companies and FTSE 100, 2000-2015

And it is not just the UK where the phenomenon can be seen – the size effect has been found all around the world, with a near-perfect inverse relationship between size and performance. In some cases, the smallest shares have beaten the largest ones by over 20% per year. Table 7.2 gives a selection of the evidence.

Study	Time period	Country/ region	Annual return of largest shares	Annual return of smallest shares
Reinganum	1963-1980	US	10% (decile)	33% (decile)
O'Shaughnessy	1951-2003	US	12% ($1bn+)	28% (<$25m)
Fama & French	1941-1990	US	12% (decile)	26% (decile)
Brown, Keim, Kleidon & Marsh	1958-1981	Australia	12% (decile)	81% (decile)
Levis & Moxon	1956-1987	UK	11% (decile)	22% (decile)
Berges, McConnell & Schlarbaum	1951-1972	Canada	11% (quintile)	24% (quintile)
Chan, Hamao & Lakonishok	1971-1998	Japan	18% (quartile)	29% (quartile)
Nakamura & Terada	1966-1983	Japan	14% (quintile)	24% (quintile)
Fama & French	1987-1995	Emerging markets	23% (half)	32% (half)

Table 7.2. Summary of evidence for small shares beating large shares

Clearly, when combined with the power of compounding, the excess returns are remarkable. For example, had you been able to invest a notional $10,000 over 17 years with 33% annual returns (as in the Reinganum study), you would end up with nearly $1.25m!

However, there are caveats. Firstly, these studies ignore transaction costs – which can be much higher among very small companies. Secondly, in some cases it would have been impossible to invest even a modest amount in these companies, because the trading volumes were so small.

Thirdly, in spite of the long-term success of the size effect, there can be long periods when it does not work at all. For example, small companies did much worse than large companies through the 1990s. To get the benefits, you have to be patient and committed.

Reasons for the size effect

Even with the caveats just mentioned, the size effect can be an incredibly powerful tool for long-term investors willing and able to exploit it. Most importantly, it is likely that the size effect will continue to reward investors, because the reasons behind it remain very much intact. It is worth looking briefly at those reasons below.

Institutional demands

Most of the money invested in stock markets is invested by large institutions. These large institutions tend to run large funds on behalf of clients who demand instant access to their money. This makes it difficult or impossible for them to invest in smaller or less liquid companies. The result is lower demand for smaller companies and higher demand for the biggest ones, leading to a discount in these smaller companies that can be exploited by those investors who can be more flexible.

Note that it is perfectly possible for even relatively large institutional managers to invest in small-cap opportunities and many do so. However, it requires careful design and implementation of the investment mandate. For example: allowing the manager to hold a long tail of small positions; using limit orders to build positions gradually; imposing side-pockets or limits on client withdrawals; and avoiding arbitrary or standardised size or liquidity constraints.

Volatility and higher required returns

The share prices of smaller companies tend to be more volatile than those of larger ones. Because investors dislike volatility, they will normally demand a higher expected return for smaller companies. For example, an investor who might be willing to buy a large company on an earnings yield of 8%, might demand an earnings yield of 10%

for a similar but smaller peer. This creates a self-fulfilling prophecy, as the lower valuations lead to higher subsequent returns.

Better shareholder alignment

It is more common for smaller companies to be run by managements with significant shareholdings, such as founder- or family-controlled businesses. In addition, smaller companies often have more concentrated shareholder bases.

Businesses with owner-managers usually enjoy better governance and higher returns than companies with a disparate shareholder base.

Fewer diseconomies of scale and greater flexibility

While many businessmen talk about economies of scale in order to emphasise the value of expansion, relatively few ever discuss *dis*economies of scale. Yet in practice, diseconomies of scale are often far more powerful than the theoretical benefits of increased size. Diseconomies of scale encompass a wide range of headwinds that all large or expanding companies have to contend with. They include things like growing bureaucracy, demotivated staff, lower R&D productivity, communication breakdowns (too many layers), inflexibility and taking a long time to adapt, and public and government opposition. In short, big companies lose *something*.

Scale can be especially dangerous in rapidly changing industries, such as tech-related businesses. Because it is especially hard for large companies to remain adaptive and creative, they will often lose out to much smaller companies as the market changes around them.

Diseconomies of scale are always a drag on growing companies and at some point they overwhelm the benefits. Often it is just sheer size that halts large companies in their tracks.

Better growth prospects

Smaller companies tend to have smaller market shares of existing markets or operate in very immature markets. Combined with fewer diseconomies of scale, this gives them superior growth potential.

Size plus value – an especially potent combination

Many studies from around the world have found that shares which are both small and lowly-valued deliver very high long-run returns, and significantly higher than smaller companies generally.[66] Chart 7.3 shows higher returns among small and micro cap value shares compared to large caps.

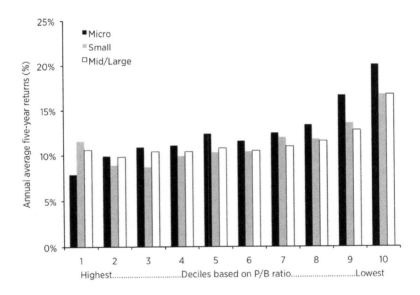

Chart 7.3. Higher returns among small and micro cap value shares[67]

---

66. As most value studies also consider the size effect separately, there is a mountain of evidence on the success of small cap value investing. See for example: Fama, E. and French, K. R., 'The Cross-Section of Expected Stock Returns', *Journal of Finance* 47:2 (1992), pp. 427-465; Chan, L. K. C., Hamao, Y. and Lakonishok, J., 'Fundamentals and Stock Returns in Japan', *Journal of Finance* 46:5 (1991), pp. 1739-1764; Basu, S., Investment Performance of Common Stocks in Relation to Their Price-Earnings Ratios: A Test of the Efficient Markets Hypothesis', *Journal of Finance* 32:3 (1977), pp. 663-682; Fama, E. F. and French, K. R., 'Value Versus Growth: The International Evidence', *Journal of Finance* 53:6 (1998), pp. 1975-1999.

67. 'The Next Big Thing Could Be Really Small: An Introduction to Global

This should come as no surprise. Really beaten-up and oversold shares will often end up small after such a big fall, and the most extreme valuations occur in the small companies that everyone else neglects. In the small-cap arena it is often not that rare to find good quality businesses that trade on low-single-digit P/Es. Such opportunities almost never occur among very large companies, simply because there are so many people watching them.

For long-term value investors, there is yet another attractive feature of smaller companies: their volatility. Small caps have historically proven more volatile than large caps. This is partly a function of markets (less liquidity leads to greater swings as investors try to move in and out) and partly due to the underlying businesses (more volatile operations and narrower access to financing).

The bigger swings in price make it easier for level-headed investors to buy really low and sell really high. To do this effectively, flexibility in terms of size is really important: as a company becomes cheaper, it will also become smaller, so you want to be able to keep adding to your holding as this happens.

A final, appealing feature among small caps is that they tend to be less well covered by other investors. It is very difficult to gain an edge when researching a mega-cap whose every action is followed by hundreds of professional analysts. By contrast, smaller companies are more likely to be under-researched, making it easier to add value through thoughtful research and analysis.

Financial strength is even more critical with smaller companies

When it comes to smaller companies, financial strength is *even more* important than usual. This is because smaller companies tend to be less diversified – both geographically and operationally – than large caps, and therefore tend to experience more volatility in their operations. Moreover, it is often much harder for smaller companies to access funding sources (such as bank loans), or at least to access them at

Micro-Cap Stocks' (The Brandes Institute, August 2014), available online at www.brandes.com/institute/research.

attractive rates. For these reasons, when investing in smaller companies, focusing on those with the strongest solvency and liquidity positions is critical.[68]

7.3 Summary

- Invest globally. Don't be biased to your home region or wherever is fashionable. Instead, go where the value is. Hunting in lowly valued (especially low-CAPE) markets usually proves extremely rewarding.

- Don't worry about currency swings. In the long run they'll come out in the wash and may well be beneficial for value investors.

- Search among and invest in smaller companies as well. Value investing is particularly effective among smaller shares, especially when accompanied by financial strength.

- For professional investors, investing in small-caps may require careful design of the investment strategy. For example: be willing to hold a long tail of small positions; use limit orders to build positions gradually; consider imposing side-pockets or liquidity restrictions on clients; and avoid arbitrary or standardised size or liquidity constraints.

- Value investors can significantly enhance returns if they can exploit volatility: rebalancing out of shares that have become expensive and popular, and building positions in undervalued and unfavoured issues.

---

68. Piotroski, J. D., 'Value Investing: The Use of Historical Financial Statement Information to Separate Winners from Losers', *Journal of Accounting Research* 38 Supplement (2000); Goldstein, M. L. and Cho, B., 'Finding Small-Capitalization Turnaround Situations That Work' (Empirical Research Partners LLC, June 2003).

CHAPTER 8.

Constructing and Managing a Portfolio

8.1 Portfolio construction

Successful long-term investing involves more than just going out and buying a bunch of your favourite shares. It is also necessary to make sure you have the right number of shares, and that those shares are sufficiently different, such that you are not exposing yourself to too much risk, i.e. putting all your eggs in one basket. In addition, you have to consider when to accumulate more shares or sell them when the price or the investment case changes.

This is the art of portfolio construction and it is a vital part of any sound investment strategy. As well as complementing the strategy's approach, portfolio construction can help mitigate risks and enforce good habits.

How many shares should be in the portfolio?

The first thing to consider is roughly how many shares you would like to own in your portfolio. There is no easy answer to this. For example, there are some highly successful investors (such as Warren Buffett) who advocate concentrated portfolios of 15 or 20 shares and there are others (such as Walter Schloss) who were happy to hold 100 or more. Peter Lynch (who delivered outstanding returns at Fidelity's Magellan Fund) held as many as 1200!

As a minimum, your portfolio should consist of at least 15 shares. The reason for having some diversification is that it is likely that many of your investments will not work out. Even the world's most successful investors typically have hit rates as low as 40% to 60%. Hard work and diligence is unfortunately not a complete defence against misfortune. The inherent uncertainties faced by economies, markets and businesses overwhelm even the most prudent investors now and again. So if you held, say, three or four shares, you could easily get unlucky and see your whole portfolio wiped out. But it is not just financial risks: highly concentrated portfolios can be very uncomfortable to hold during volatile periods.

In deciding how many shares to hold, there are a number of factors to consider, which I discuss below.

Tolerance for risk and volatility

The more shares you have, the less your portfolio will be influenced by the volatility of each individual share. Thus, a more diversified portfolio is likely to be less volatile overall. From an emotional perspective this can be very important. You don't want a portfolio that is so volatile it is going to cause you too much anxiety. This is especially important amongst contrarian or value shares, where there are often negative headlines and problems that have to be worked through. It is much easier to live with a 0.5% or 1% position that is having problems than it is with a 5% or 10% position.

How much time you require to research and monitor each share

Research approaches to investments vary enormously. Some investors are happy to pick shares after a few hours' work, others require several weeks or even months. Clearly, the number of shares you can review and keep track of will limit the size of your portfolio. If you're a very in-depth investor, a small number is preferable. Those with a more cursory approach may wish to hold more.

The time and resources available

It is not just a question of how much time is required for each share, but how much time you have to spend. Peter Lynch was able to hold over a thousand shares because he was a full-time investor with dozens of research analysts supporting him. Conversely, if you're an individual investor with a full-time job, you may only have a few hours a week to spare. Those with less time and research resources should focus on a smaller number of shares.

Size and liquidity constraints

We have already seen how buying into smaller companies can do wonders for investors' returns. Unfortunately, investing in these can be more difficult for institutional investors or very wealthy investors with a lot of money to invest. In this case, it may be necessary to hold more shares (meaning a smaller amount of money needs to be invested in each one). This can be done by making all position sizes small, or having smaller position sizes for smaller companies.

In practice, most investors find their appropriate number of shares more by accident than by design. It tends to evolve over time and then naturally settle within a certain range. However, if you are just starting out, it is worthwhile noting the above considerations and having a rough idea, so you can set your position sizes appropriately.

Setting limits: the need for a risk framework

Simply holding a large number of shares does not guarantee sufficient diversification. This is because the shares you select may be exposed to the same themes or events. For example, holding 20 US banks may provide less diversification than holding three or four genuinely different companies, because the US banks may be exposed to the same economic happenings.

In order to ensure sufficient diversification, it is prudent to set out a risk framework. A risk framework limits exposure to any particular share, industry or country, thereby mitigating risks. Professional investors will be familiar with risk frameworks as they are always a requirement. For individual investors they can be a very good idea as well.

A basic risk framework should include:

- The minimum number of shares you will hold in the portfolio.

- The maximum size of any single position as a percentage of the overall portfolio value.

- The maximum exposure to any single country or region as a percentage of the overall portfolio value.

- The maximum exposure to any industry or sector as a percentage of the overall portfolio value.

In addition, when defining your risk framework I would suggest the following tips:

- **Keep it simple.** There are all sorts of complex formulae available for measuring risk (such as tracking error, beta or effective number of shares). These are normally too complicated to really help you understand what is going on in your portfolio, and can often be misleading. They can also be difficult to calculate. Instead, set simple absolute limits that you can check at a glance.

- **Go for absolute limits, not relative limits.** Many investors set limits by comparing their portfolio to a broad index. This can be dangerous, as sectors or countries can go through bubbles or busts. Relative limits may force you to buy into bubbles (as a country or industry becomes an increasingly large part of the index) or to sell out in deep bear markets when you should be buying (because that country or sector has become a small part of the index).

- **Give yourself enough room to be active.** Successful investing demands the willingness and ability to run a truly differentiated portfolio that reflects an investor's strongest convictions. So make sure your risk framework is not so restrictive that you cannot take meaningful positions in companies, industries, economies or themes where you find major opportunities; or that it forces you into cutting your positions too early when those investments begin to appreciate.

The following list is an example of the risk framework I follow for my own fund:

- Minimum of 60 shares.

- Maximum individual holding size of 10% of the fund's total value and positions of 5% or more should not aggregate to more than 40% of the fund's total value.

- The portfolio should have no more than one-third (33.3%) of its total value invested in any single GICS (Global Industry Classification Standard) sector.

- The portfolio should contain shares from a minimum of six countries; with no more than 30% in any developed country other than the US (50%), and no more than 20% in any emerging market.

Having formulated a risk framework, make sure you stick to it! It can be very tempting to tweak the framework when things go well and positions appreciate, often bumping up against the limits. This is exactly the point when it is imperative to stick to your risk framework.

If you feel it is really necessary to make changes to your risk framework, this is best done during a period of difficult performance, when your outlook will be risk averse rather than reckless.

Be wary of hidden themes

Unfortunately, even a well considered risk framework may not be enough to ensure a balanced portfolio. This is because disparate companies spread across different countries and industries may still be exposed to the same themes or events. For example, during the global financial crisis, Greek Banks, Irish house-builders and American car-makers tumbled together, because all of them were exposed to the bursting of the credit bubble among Western consumers. More recently, countries as diverse as Australia and Brazil have seen their economies move down in lockstep due to their dependence on Chinese commodity demand.

While inadvertent exposure to themes like this can be dangerous, there is no sure-fire way to identify them. There are however two things you can do to help.

The first is to imagine some major economic scenarios, such as interest rates double, the US goes into a recession, a major terrorist attack, or commodity prices halve. Now look through your portfolio, and as you do so, question whether your portfolio may be disproportionately vulnerable to any of them.

A second exercise is to discuss your portfolio with other investors and ask what themes they would be worried about. When it comes to managing risk, the more different the investors are to you, the better. Investors with different perspectives are more likely to spot the very risks that you will overlook.

If you do identify significant exposure to hidden themes, consider reducing that exposure or not adding any more to it. At the very least make sure you are comfortable with the position you are taking.

8.2 Buying discipline

Volatility is the value investor's best friend

The great thing about shares is that they're so volatile and there are lots of them. Look in a newspaper at 52-week highs and lows and you'll see that most shares move up or down 50% or more over the course of a year. It is this volatility that is so valuable for the long-term investor, because it means there is a constant stream of bargains (opportunities to buy low) and shares rising to their full worth or more (opportunities to sell high).

To exploit this volatility, all you need to do is to find a reasonably sensible way to analyse companies and roughly value them. Then just keep buying those at the biggest discounts and selling them on when the discount vanishes.

It is unlikely that you will look at a company just at the point you want to invest in it. So you should keep following businesses after you have analysed them, with a valuation (either a price or a multiple) in mind. It may take years, but patient diligence is normally rewarded with an ideal entry point. When you do buy, it is worth holding back a bit, so you can add to your position if the share gets even cheaper.

This all seems eminently sensible. It is simply the method for buying low and selling high. But as we'll see in the next chapter, very few investors manage to do this. The main difficulty with effective value investing is that it normally means appearing wrong for a while. Identifying when the herd is doing the wrong thing and going against it is not enough. Usually the euphoria or excessive pessimism will blithely continue, possibly for a long time. As Howard Marks explains:

> "The contrarian will appear wrong, and the fact that his error comes in acting differently will make him look like an oddball loser. Thus successful contrarianism requires the ability to stick with losing positions that frequently appear imprudent in the eyes of conventional wisdom."[69]

The importance of rebalancing and averaging down

Rebalancing a value portfolio involves consistently selling out of shares that have gone up and become richly valued, and reinvesting the proceeds into the new generation of undervalued dogs. This is a critical part of value investing and the main driver of value's superior returns.

---

69. Marks, H., 'Memo to Clients: Ditto' (Oaktree Capital Management, L. P., January 2013).

A fantastic piece of recent research found that annual rebalancing was the key contributor to the success of value strategies across the world.[70] This is because, with each rebalance, the value investor is exchanging something with a high valuation and a low yield for something with a lower valuation and higher yield – with each rebalance, the investor is swapping less for more.

An important aspect of rebalancing is *averaging down*, or *munching* as it is sometimes known. This involves buying more shares as the price falls. Typically, specific price points for adding to the position are set in advance, so that the investor will be gradually increasing his stake as the price falls, providing the fundamental investment case remains intact. A systematic approach to doing this is explained below. Because out-of-favour shares tend to have a lot of negative momentum, they will typically carry on falling way below what might be viewed as a bargain price, and the shrewd investor will get plenty of opportunities to increase his stake.

Munching on a share as its price falls is a common habit among leading investors. Recent research by Bruce Greenwald[71] and Jonathan Rhinesmith[72] has found that some of the world's best investment records are almost entirely a result of averaging down: that is, the vast majority of excess returns did not come from the first purchase but from later additions at lower prices.

However, it is important to emphasise that you should not just keep on buying blindly. The share may have fallen because something may have happened in the meantime that undermines the investment. So before each purchase, it is necessary to revisit the share to make sure that the investment case is still intact.

I have also found another benefit to having a strategy of averaging down. When things look ugly, it is often very tempting to try and time the market. So even if you find a truly undervalued share, you

---

70. Chaves, D. B. and Arnott, R. D., 'Rebalancing and the Value Effect', *The Journal of Portfolio Management* 38:4 (2012), pp. 59-74.

71. Greenwald, B. C. N., 'Value Investing 101', interview with The Motley Fool (August 2004).

72. Rhinesmith, J., 'Doubling Down' (June 2014), available at SSRN: ssrn.com/abstract=2491636

think, "Well, the outlook isn't great now, so I'll wait, and try to catch the bottom." However, trying to do this will often lead you to miss out entirely, as the point at which the outlook is at its worst is usually the bottom. If you have a plan for averaging down, you will be less tempted to try and be too cute with your timing, because you know you will be buying more even if you are a bit early.

As common sense goes, averaging down is up there with the best and simplest of ideas. If you have a value for something in mind (whether it be shares or anything else for that matter), you should be delighted to load up on more at ever increasing discounts to the thing's value.

A formalised approach

While rebalancing is a great idea in theory, it is rather more difficult in practice. It takes courage to add to shares as their prices fall. Furthermore, to average down the investor must have the money available to do so, and that requires a carefully planned portfolio with either cash or assets that can be readily sold.

For these reasons, I find it helps to have a mechanical system in place. A simple and easy way to do this is to use a computer spreadsheet and list all the shares you own or are considering, with columns for the current price, your assessment of intrinsic value (either a price or a multiple), and the difference between the price and your value. If you have access to platforms such as Bloomberg, you can get live updates for prices and multiples. If not you can input them manually.

Having set this up, you can use the 'Sort' function to order the shares according to their discount or premium to your valuation. In an instant you can now see which of your shares are the most attractively priced and which you are ready to sell.

You should then aim to buy more of the shares as their discount gets larger (rechecking the investment case before each addition) and sell when the discount disappears (again, rechecking your assessment beforehand).

Table 8.1 provides an illustration of this technique (remember that the exact position sizes and discount points will depend on the individual investor).

Stock	Intrinsic value	Current price	Discount to intrinsic value	Buying/selling action
Stock 1	30	5	83%	Invest £30k into each of these stocks at > 75% discount
Stock 2	250	47	81%	
Stock 3	99	23	77%	
Stock 4	768	190	75%	
Stock 5	7889	2110	73%	Invest £20k into each of these stocks at > 62.5% discount
Stock 6	36	10	72%	
Stock 7	28	9	68%	
Stock 8	56	19	66%	
Stock 9	11	4	64%	
Stock 10	123	49	60%	Invest £10k into each of these stocks at > 50% discount
Stock 11	345	147	57%	
Stock 12	678	299	56%	
Stock 13	890	401	55%	
Stock 14	450	210	53%	
Stock 15	455	224	51%	
Stock 16	34	18	47%	
Stock 17	12	7	42%	
Stock 18	8	6	25%	
Stock 19	69	54	22%	
Stock 20	78	63	19%	
Stock 21	8765	7666	13%	
Stock 22	98	86	12%	
Stock 23	11	10	9%	
Stock 24	490	484	1%	
Stock 25	29	30	-3%	If owned, sell these stocks to rebalance into any available discounted stocks
Stock 26	33	37	-12%	
Stock 27	6712	7569	-13%	
Stock 28	6	9	-50%	

Table 8.1. Example of Excel system for portfolio management

Something else I find useful is to shade in the shares as they're bought, with colours getting darker as more are bought (not shown in example). The aim is to buy gradually more of the shares with the biggest discounts, so the shading should get darker as the discount to intrinsic value widens. Then all you have to do is keep the prices up to date and recheck your assumptions before each decision.

Turning what is normally an angst-ridden and time-consuming process fraught with behavioural hang-ups into a simplistic colouring-in exercise not only makes life easier, but also encourages buy and sell habits to move closer to what is optimal.

8.3 Know when to fold 'em

Have an exit strategy

A sound approach to buying is only half the story. Entry strategies need to be paired with exit strategies. For value investors this means selling when the margin of safety (i.e. the discount to intrinsic value) closes.

Good sell discipline is likely to prove just as important to long-term results as a sound approach to buying. Unfortunately, the majority of investors do not give sell discipline its fair share of attention. This can lead to two common pitfalls.

The first is selling too soon. So an investor will see, say, a 50% gain and button up his profit right away. That is often sub-optimal. Value, like most investment approaches, relies on some very big winners. What should matter is not the profit, but the discount to intrinsic worth. In practice, value and contrarian approaches typically work best over holding periods of three to five years, with the biggest gains coming in years two to four. So selling too soon can be heavily deleterious.

The flipside is that sometimes investors fail to sell at all, getting caught up in the hype as the share rises and rises, only to then be left watching it fall back to earth again. This is known as *round-tripping*.

Just as no investor can hope to buy at the bottom, nor can they hope to sell exactly at the top. The best defence against premature selling or round-tripping is to set a valuation or multiple that you feel reflects fair value *at the time of buying*. This does not mean you should sell automatically as soon as the share gets there. Things might have changed with the passage of time. However, having set that valuation, it should act as a trigger to revisit the investment with a *seller's mindset* – i.e. looking for the appropriate exit point.

Good sell discipline also leads to low turnover, meaning less work and lower costs. This is because it will typically take several years for a large margin of safety to close. If you find yourself trading too much, simply widen your required margin of safety. That way you will find less to buy and you will be waiting longer on average before each sale.

When things don't work out

The world we live in is hugely unpredictable and constantly changing. You can find the perfect share, check everything diligently, and still end up with a loss. Even the most brilliant investors suffer many investments that fail.

Shares that appear cheap and subsequently do badly are often referred to as *value traps*. Getting out of a value trap is the smartest thing to do, but it can also be one of the hardest. No one likes to take a loss – it's an unpleasant thing to do, even when it is the right thing. The temptation is often to irrationally hang on to a failing investment hoping something good comes along. Moreover, it can be very hard to distinguish between value traps (that should be sold) and shares that are just getting cheaper (and should be added to).

There are no easy answers. However, it is worth being mindful of the most common causes of value traps. These are instances where it is normally appropriate to sell immediately, even if that means taking a loss. I discuss these below.

Rapidly deteriorating financials

This is the most common cause of value traps. Financial problems tend to rapidly spiral out of control as everyone (customers, creditors, lenders) loses confidence at once. It is therefore important to sell quickly.

You were wrong

Now and again you are likely to find that you have bought something based on an investment case that is simply incorrect. Perhaps you got the numbers confused, or overestimated the potential market. Everyone makes mistakes. Sell up, move on and learn from it.

Obliteration

Something very big and very bad happens at the company. Perhaps it loses a key patent battle, its sole customer goes bust, or its main asset is expropriated. Clearly, these sort of events will destroy a large part of a company's true value. In such an instance, revisit the investment and sell quickly and decisively. Loss aversion among other investors will mean you often get a chance to get out at a modest loss before the shares really tank.

Obsolescence

Investment cases are typically based on the premise that the business can continue to operate in much the same way as it has in the past. However, this is rarely the case and a problem companies often face is that their core products become obsolete. A good example is Kodak – the maker of photographic films – which was bankrupted by the growth of digital photography.

The important thing about obsolescence is that you cannot extrapolate. A disruptive technology may gain traction only slowly and then suddenly burst into rapid growth. At first it may seem like a minor threat and then it can completely take over. For instance, mobile telephony was around for two decades before it suddenly smashed the market for landlines.

Moreover, profitability may disappear faster than demand as the company cannot cut its costs fast enough, or where there are large legacy liabilities. This is what has destroyed many newspapers: even where the internet has only hurt demand modestly, they still require the same cost base. Worse still, liabilities that can seem manageable for a growing company can become overwhelming when that company goes into decline.

Even where declining companies remain financially viable, another risk is that they waste money trying to diversify into other areas, often through expensive acquisitions.

This is not to say declining businesses cannot be sound investments. However, they need to be monitored very carefully and disruptive threats should be taken seriously.

8.4 Summary

- Make sure your portfolio is sufficiently diversified. Diversification is necessary to mitigate financial risks and psychological discomfort during the inevitable periods when your investments are performing poorly.

- A simple risk framework is helpful in maintaining an adequately diversified portfolio, providing you stick to it. In addition, consider a broad range of potential economic scenarios and seek out alternative investor perspectives to check for hidden risks.

- Value investors can significantly enhance returns if they can exploit volatility: rebalancing out of shares that have become expensive and popular, and building positions in undervalued and unfavoured issues.

- The best way to take advantage of volatility is to apply a formalised and disciplined approach. Keep a spreadsheet and sort shares by discounts to fair value, with specific points for adding and selling. Always revisit a share before buying, adding or selling to make sure the investment case is still as you think it is.

- Good selling is just as important as good buying – don't neglect it.

- Have an intrinsic value in mind from the time of buying. Sell decisions should be based on the intrinsic value, when the margin of safety disappears.

- If you get into a value trap, do not dither. Sell quickly and decisively, and learn from it.

PART IV.

Implementation

CHAPTER 9

Winning in Practice

"If you set out to take Vienna, take Vienna!"

Napoleon

9.1 Mind the empathy gap

"The investor's chief problem — and even his worst enemy — is likely to be himself."

Benjamin Graham

Value investing beats value investors

In 2009, legendary value investor Joel Greenblatt set up the Magic Formula Investing Fund to help individuals invest using his well-known Magic Formula.

As we saw in Chapter 5, the Magic Formula is a very simple system for selecting value shares with low EV/EBIT multiples and which are earning high returns on capital. Investors using the platform were given two choices. The first option was to have their money invested with the shares picked and weighted mechanically, according to the formula. The second option was a discretionary account, whereby customers could select their choice of shares from the list of Magic Formula shares, and choose when to buy and sell them.

After two years, the robotic formula had beaten the S&P 500 by over 21%, while the average discretionary account (selecting from the same list of shares remember), had underperformed by more than 3%. Human input managed to destroy a whopping 24% of returns in two years.[73] The discretionary investors churned their portfolios, buying the shares after they'd done well and selling them after they did poorly. In short, human judgment took a very good strategy and turned it into a bad one.

Anyone who has seen even a few back-tests of simple value strategies (such as low P/B or low P/E investing), cannot help but notice this. These simple robotic back-tests have typically demonstrated outperformance of 5% to 20% per annum. They require nothing more than primary school arithmetic. And yet, of the thousands of sophisticated funds that claim to practice value investing, only a tiny handful – certainly less than 5% – have delivered long-run outperformance of even 1% to 2%. Value investing beats value investors!

Why value investors fail

Why do investors fail to do what they set out to do?

There are two fundamental reasons.

The first is to do with how our brains make decisions. Over the past 50 years, scientists have found an enormous range of biases, shortcuts and subconscious quirks in human decision-making. They include

---

73. Greenblatt, J., 'Adding Your Two Cents May Cost You A Lot Over The Long Term', Joel's Column (January 2012), available online at: xat-www. magicformulainvesting.inautix.com/joel_column.html

things like being disproportionately influenced by very recent events, over-extrapolating historic trends or doing things because other people are also doing them. It is these instincts that cause most investors to execute poorly.

The second reason – affecting professional investors but not individual investors – is what Warren Buffett has called "the institutional imperative." This is where institutional investors act in ways that are ultimately bad for investment returns, but good for their business.

For example, they may sell unpopular but undervalued shares because they do not want the hassle of having worried clients. Or they may buy overvalued, fashionable shares because they are more presentable. Or, as we have seen already, they may try to herd, delivering mediocre performance with a low risk of standing out. In addition, institutional structures are rarely suited to the courageous sort of decisions that true value investors need to make. Often there are large teams or committees with several layers of managers involved. This makes it difficult to invest in controversial or contrarian shares.

Taken together, these pressures make investing much harder in practice than in theory, just as a footballer finds it much harder to slot away a penalty kick in a big match than during practice. The fact that so many investors – perhaps more than 99% – fail to execute, illustrates how powerful these forces are, and how easy it is to underestimate them. Even the tiny minority who do succeed face a constant struggle.

In order to succeed, it is first necessary to understand why value works so effectively. Value investing works by exploiting the instincts and habits of the majority – i.e. it works by not doing what people want to do. So whatever you do, you must not let those impulses in the back door, as most investors do. When value investors fail, it is because they make the mistake of thinking it is their skills and insights that create the value; in fact, it is the system.

This chapter is all about executing well. If you cannot follow the system consistently, value investing cannot work its magic.

9.2 The three biggest obstacles for investors

The three biggest obstacles preventing investors from executing effectively are:

1. the pull of the herd

2. outcome bias

3. unmanageable complexity

1. The pull of the herd

Many people imagine value investors to be lone contrarians, their actions a world away from the market's. While a few well-known investors may live up to this stereotype, most do not.

In a fascinating paper, Amil Dasgupta examined the trading habits of thousands of American institutional investors.[74] He found that it didn't really matter whether the managers defined themselves as 'growth' or 'value'; they almost all behaved pretty much the same way, buying and selling the same stuff at the same time.

Moreover, what they bought was predictable – large, liquid, expensive, momentum shares. He also found a near-perfect negative correlation between their buying and selling habits and subsequent returns. Over the subsequent two years, the top decile of Dasgupta's *sheep index* (the shares they were all buying) underperformed by 6% while the bottom decile (the shares they were all selling) outperformed by 17%.

For anyone familiar with behavioural psychology, this is not much of a surprise. Herding is the most powerful behavioural instinct we have and infects every aspect of our lives. The herd instinct – i.e. the urge to copy the behaviour of those around us – is deeply rooted in our psyche. Ancient humans simply could not survive on their own, outside of a tribe, so fitting in and learning from others became a hardwired

---

74. Dasgupta, A., Prat, A. and Verardo, M., 'The Price of Conformism' (2005), available online at: www.econ.yale.edu/~shiller/behfin/2006-04/ dasgupta-prat-verardo.pdf

survival instinct. Even in the modern world, herding is still a good idea most of the time. We learn and develop by copying others, and life is normally easier when we fit in and agree with those around us.

Given all this, it is no surprise how much herding influences our behaviour, even if subconsciously. Things like the clothes we wear, the music we listen to, our political opinions, and so on, are mainly determined by those around us.

In financial markets herding is only getting worse. For starters, modern technology is binding the world's investors closer and closer together – no matter where they are, everyone is receiving the same information and opinions at the same time. And as we have seen, the growing influence of institutions exacerbates herd-like behaviour.

But I think there is a third reason why herding is on the rise and that is the expansion of education. More people are in formal education than ever before and students today spend longer in education than ever before. For all the benefits of mass education, it can only function by encouraging and rewarding conformity – it is simply not possible to run a school or college with every individual doing their own thing. Further, professional finance tends to recruit the most highly qualified students – i.e. those who have succeeded in institutional education. Ironically, by selecting highly educated graduates, financial institutions may actually be filling up with those most prone to herding.

2. Outcome bias

Outcome bias is the habit of judging a decision by its outcome rather than the quality of the decision at the time it was made. For example, if you buy a share and the next day a freak accident destroys the main factory, that is not something you could have foreseen. Good and bad luck can, of course, cut both ways. There are an awful lot of things in the world that we just cannot predict. The upshot is that, for investors, short-term results are determined more by luck than by judgment.

While herding may be the most powerful instinct, the temptation to focus on recent results is probably the most difficult behavioural bias to avoid. Again, technological advances have made things even harder. With modern computing, we can get investment results any second of the day, making the pressure to focus on those short-term outcomes even greater.

Unfortunately, focusing on short-term outcomes rather than the decision-making process leads to a variety of problems. Most commonly, an unlucky streak of bad results can lead an investor to jettison a sensible approach. Alternatively, an exceptionally good period may encourage the investor to break away from their plan, to use more discretion and to take more risks.

Value investors are *especially* at risk of outcome bias. The fact that value strategies often do poorly early on (at the time the decisions are fresh in the investor's mind), means there is a lot of pressure to give up or make unhelpful changes. Moreover, the soundest value strategies also tend to be quite simplistic, so it can be tempting to swap them for something more sophisticated.

Instead, investors need to focus on their process and *not* on the outcomes. First and foremost, this means constantly making sure you are executing fully and consistently. This is logical: the process is the bit we can control, the outcomes are not.

Now and again, it is important to review the process and carefully go through where you got things wrong. But this should be done when you are relaxed and things are going well. The pressure to change your process always builds when results are poor, so this is exactly not the time to be making major alterations, as you cannot hope to take a balanced view.

The legendary value manager Seth Klarman summed it up beautifully when he wrote:

> "You may find it surprising that when we purchase a bond or a stock we are not directly trying to make money. Rather, we are trying to apply a sound process in order to make a good investment decision, which will then result in our making money. The essential difference is that when investors single-mindedly attempt to make money, they often try too hard. This leads them to focus on the near-term direction of a particular security or the overall market (which we believe is unknowable). They may impatiently or greedily assume unacceptable levels of

risk, and perhaps justify their decisions by stretching criteria or confusing belief with knowledge."[75]

This wonderfully simple diagram by Carl Richards illustrates how investors should confine their focus.[76]

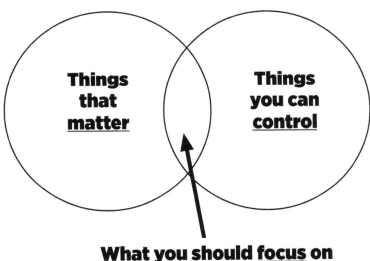

What you should <u>focus</u> on

3. Unmanageable complexity

In 1935 Boeing were bidding for a large government aircraft contract. Their plane – the Model 299 (the predecessor to the B17) – was the most sophisticated aircraft ever built and miles ahead of the competition. It was seen as a shoo-in for the contract. However, on the demonstration day, a simple pilot error caused the 299 to crash and the loss nearly bankrupted the company. The problem was that Boeing's advancements in technology and sophistication had made

---

75. Klarman, S. A., 'Letter to Shareholders' (2009).
76. Richards, C., *The One-Page Financial Plan: A Simple Way to Be Smart About Your Money* (Portfolio, 2015).

the plane too complicated for even the best pilots. The press dubbed it "Too much airplane for one man to fly."

This is the downside risk of technological progress. Rapid advancements in speed and sophistication lead to exponential increases in the number of possible errors. Of course, the problem is not confined to aviation. In fact, almost every role has seen an explosion in complexity over the past century and it shows no sign of slowing down. The result is that many tasks have morphed from jobs that required skill and experience into an art of managing extreme complexity. As Atul Gawande has observed, "Much of our work today has entered its own B17 phase... Multiple fields have become too much airplane for one person to fly."[77]

As well as making execution more difficult, complexity can get in the way of decision-making. Quantities of information and the speed at which it flows have also grown exponentially. As Malcolm Gladwell has observed:

> "We have virtually unlimited amounts of data at our fingertips, and we're all versed in arguments about the dangers of not knowing enough and not doing our homework. But what I have sensed is an enormous frustration with the unexpected costs of knowing too much. We have come to confuse information and understanding. The key to good decision-making is not knowledge. It is understanding. We are swimming in the former. We are desperately lacking in the latter."[78]

In a fascinating study of horse racing experts, pundits were asked to predict race results based on items of information they were given. Initially they were given just five items, with the number rising to as many as 40 items.[79] Although their confidence rose with the amount of information, their predictions actually got slightly worse. Many similar studies have been conducted across a wide range of fields and have all

---

77. Gawande, A., *The Checklist Manifesto: How to Get Things Right* (London: Profile Books, 2010) p. 34.

78. Gladwell, M., *Blink: The Power of Thinking Without Thinking* (New York: Little, Brown & Co, 2005), p. 264.

79. Slovic, P., 'Behavioural Problems of Adhering to a Decision Policy', Paper presented at the Institute for Quantitative Research in Finance Napa, CA. (May 1973).

reached the same conclusion: beyond five or six items of information, experts' confidence goes up while the quality of their decisions goes down.[80]

The problem is that even the very best human brains struggle to manage highly complex tasks, or to interpret large amounts of data. And this becomes even more difficult in environments of rapid change or high pressure. Under such conditions, most simply fall back on their instincts.

Investing is patently an area which has witnessed exactly this sort of exponential growth in complexity and news-flow. For value investors, complexity represents yet another hurdle to overcome. In getting bogged down in complexity or news-flow, value investors stop getting the basics right consistently. It is at this point that value investing stops working.

Like other fields that can become overwhelmed by complexity, it is vital for investors to identify what they believe to be the most important elements of the investment strategy, and to make sure they follow them consistently. This may be as simple as having a list of three or four 'must have' criteria that all new investments must meet.

---

80. Goldberg, L. R., 'Simple Models or Simple Processes? Some Research on Clinical Judgments', *American Psychologist* 23:7 (1968), pp. 483-496.

9.3 Execution: have a simple plan

"The greatest enemy of a good plan is the dream of a perfect plan."

Carl von Clausewitz, *On War* (1832)

To reiterate, the principles of value investing work, providing they are consistently followed. Success lies in the consistent adherence to a sound process, not in the intelligence of the investor. For this reason, value investing won't do much for an investor's ego. Just appreciating this is a huge achievement.

In the last section, we saw how various factors can make it very hard to perform value investing. In particular, more complicated processes tend to end in more mistakes, while more information will generally lead to worse decisions rather than better ones. Moreover, value investing works by exploiting the instinctive (but incorrect) actions of other investors – it is supposed to feel awkward.

On top of all this, there is the environment. A pressured or changing environment can make doing the simplest tasks very difficult. In medicine, one of the most commonplace tasks is inserting an intravenous line into a patient. There are five steps to inserting an intravenous line and it is very important they are followed. Not doing the steps correctly can lead to infection and even death. Nurses and doctors who do this are highly trained and understand the importance of following the steps.

And yet, studies have found that even experienced physicians get it wrong about 30% of the time. It is not down to stupidity or difficulty, it is just very hard to follow any sort of system in chaotic situations such as operating theatres. The fact that highly trained people in life-or-death situations cannot get a five-step procedure right shows how difficult consistent execution is under pressure. Investors face much the same problem.

All this means that consistently executing a value investing strategy is very, very difficult. However, there are three things an investor can do right from the start to make it easier:

1. invest a lot of time up front in making a plan

2. keep it really simple and really clear

3. focus on your execution and not on your results

1. Invest a lot of time up front in making a plan

It's a lot easier to follow a plan that you trust. By investing a lot of time and effort in getting it right you are much more likely to stick to it. So start by taking the time to think a lot and read a lot. Devise a plan which plays to your personal strengths and the values you stand for. It may be that you end up rejecting value investing for something else that is more suited to you – so be it.

2. Keep it really simple and really clear

It is much easier to follow a simple plan than a complex one. The fact that very simple value strategies consistently beat sophisticated investors shows that things do not need to be complicated. One or two points may be enough.

As well as being simple, make your plan as clear and precise as possible. Once again, it is much easier under pressure to follow something that is unambiguous.

Try some of these exercises to help define what really matters to your plan:

- You have to build your portfolio with only six pieces of information on any share. What would those six things be?

- You have to hand your portfolio over to a 12-year-old. What instructions do you give her?

- You have one day (or one hour) a month to invest. How are you going to use it?

- Try writing your process on the back of a postcard.

3. Focus on your execution and not on your results

Once you have built your simple, clear and thoughtful plan, it is time to start following it. For at least several years, the results will tell you little or nothing about your investing prowess and a lot about how lucky you are. Looking at performance *cannot* help you, but it might hinder or upset you. So avoid giving it any attention – there is only downside from trying to measure short-term performance.

Instead, focus on how consistently you are following your plan. Take time to regularly check yourself. If you do feel you are getting despondent, remember that the best opportunities for most strategies are generally after a bad prolonged period. And remember Churchill's advice: "If you're going through hell, keep going!"

9.4 The checklist revolution

What are checklists?

A checklist is simply a list of tasks that you follow in a set order. As you complete each task, you (mentally or literally) tick it off, and move on to the next.

Checklists first became popular in the airline industry. As planes became more complicated, it became easy to make routine errors which could end in disaster. By specifying the fundamental steps required for each manoeuvre, pilots were far less likely to miss things out or to do them in the wrong order.

Following a checklist is not the same as acting like a robot. A checklist will not complete tasks or make judgments for you. There is still a lot of skill and input required. Hence, a pilot must decide what checklist to use and when, and must then use his or her skills and judgment to complete each step properly, as well as adding other steps where appropriate.

Because checklists have proved so incredibly effective, they are increasingly being used across a range of industries, from medicine to construction. They are also being used by a tiny minority of investors, some of whom are reporting stunning results.

For example, a study of venture capital investors[81] found that the small number who used checklists as a core component of their framework enjoyed median returns of 80%, versus 35% for those relying on more instinctive approaches.

Why are checklists so great?

Checklists work

The brilliance of checklists was summed up perfectly by one investor when he said, "When surgeons make sure to wash their hands or to talk to everyone on the team, they improve their outcomes with no increase in skill. That's what we are doing when we use the checklist."[82] Checklists can make surgeons, pilots or investors better at their jobs without the need for more talent, intelligence, experience, time or resources.

They do this by making sure we do what we already *know* we should do. As we've already seen, simply executing basic tasks can be brutally hard. By making sure we get those basic steps right every time, a humble checklist gives an enormous leap in performance.

Investing is a great place for checklists, because there is so much scope for missteps and misjudgments. It is not just that investing is complex, but also because the sort of impulsive reactions investors tend to make can be so damaging.

Charlie Munger once observed, "It is remarkable how much long-term advantage people like us have gotten by trying to be consistently not

81. Smart, G. H., 'Management Assessment Methods in Venture Capital: An Empirical Analysis of Human Capital Valuation', *Journal of Private Equity* 2:3 (1999), pp. 29-45.
82. Gawande, A., *The Checklist Manifesto: How to Get Things Right* (London: Profile Books, 2010), p. 168.

stupid, instead of trying to be very intelligent."[83] This is exactly what checklists can do. As one checklist fan explained: "They provide a cognitive net. They catch the mental flaws in all of us."[84]

Checklists work in chaotic, complex and pressured situations

It is perhaps not surprising that checklists are becoming popular with surgeons. Surgery is a great place to use checklists because things rarely go as planned: there are often delays, complications and distractions as well as the intense pressure. This means simple things that could prove fatal (like washing hands) can easily get missed.

While investing may not be life-or-death, the pressures and constant surprises of the stock market mean simple mistakes are just as likely. This is where the checklist really comes into its own. Instead of being paralysed by fear or overwhelmed by complexity, an investor can turn to his checklist for support. The checklist provides a starting point and it also prevents the most dangerous mistakes. Most importantly, it focuses the investor on the fundamentals of the process, and away from the noise and mood-swings of Mr Market. The checklist removes the investor from the herd. I have found working through checklists in panic-ridden markets or shares to be a strangely calming experience.

Checklists provide a pathway to improvement

This book is all about becoming better at investing. Becoming better involves constantly checking your process, learning from others and looking out for your own mistakes. A problem many investors face is that, even when they might have an idea about how to improve, they have no way to implement it. Without a framework to build on, they cannot progress.

A checklist (or several) not only provides that basic framework, but it also provides an incredibly easy way to improve. As time goes on, you simply adjust your checklist based on the lessons you learn. So you can keep learning *and* keep improving.

---

83. Munger, C., Wesco Financial Corporation Annual Report (1989).
84. Gawande, A., *The Checklist Manifesto: How to Get Things Right* (London: Profile Books, 2010), p. 48.

Because of this convenient way to improve, checklists completely change attitudes to mistakes. Instead of mistakes being embarrassing and frustrating, they actually feel good and worthwhile. Making any mistake once is excusable and valuable. Making the same mistake twice is neither. This is the most rewarding thing about checklists: you only need to make a mistake once.

They're quick

Another advantage of checklists is that I have found they speed up the decision-making process. Using checklists enables me to reject many unsuitable ideas very quickly without wasting a lot of time and effort. Working through checklists also lets me see early on where the major points of concern are and where I need to direct more in-depth research. Moreover, as I have got into the habit of repeatedly using checklists, I have become quicker and more thorough at working through them. They have become habitual rather than a chore.

All this speed and efficiency has one big advantage – you can widen your opportunity set vastly. By having a system that enables you to work through many shares quickly and objectively regardless of the environment, you are far more likely to uncover those fantastic bargains.

They're cheap

All that is required is a piece of paper, a pencil and the time to go through the checklist.

They're adaptable

As well as being improvable, checklists can be easily adapted for different users and different situations.

They're transmissible

Changing and improving processes among checklist users is incredibly simple and quick. Atul Gawande gives an example of how it took 17 years to implement new surgical procedures to prevent a certain infection in US hospitals. Even then, it still wasn't perfect. By contrast, when airlines needed to implement a new safety procedure for planes flying over the Arctic, they simply updated the checklists, achieving 100% compliance in a matter of days.

They can improve teamwork and avoid communication breakdowns

For investors who work in teams or as part of bigger institutions, checklists have one final, very valuable benefit – they can improve communication and co-operation. A common problem in almost all corporations is communication breakdown. Without constant and clear communication, employees often end up working against each other or repeating the same tasks rather than working together. When this sort of thing is happening, people can quickly become demotivated and cease to achieve their potential. Unfortunately, the best investors are not always the best managers or the best communicators.

Checklists can get round this by having *communication tasks* specified within them. Investors can build in checks specifying who to talk to and when, and what needs to be communicated. All this can lead to a higher quality of work and a friendlier and more motivating environment, as well as helping to avoid regulatory breaches.

Creating and using checklists

A checklist can only work if the user is willing to follow it. I have seen dozens of real-life examples of investors quickly penning off checklists, only to forget about them within a week or two.

Committing to a checklist is remarkably hard. To stand a chance of sticking to it, you must really believe in your checklist. That means it should be your own. It should reflect your personal thoughts about what is most important and what is the best order for each step. Building a checklist is a deeply personal journey of learning, experience and introspection. By investing a lot of time and thought into your checklist, you will be far more likely to apply it consistently and respect it.

Even with a lot of time and thought, it is highly unlikely that you will come up with the perfect checklist right away. In my first year of using investment checklists, I was typically making one or two tweaks to them every week. So as you use your checklist, constantly think how you might improve it. These will mostly be small changes, such as adding in an extra check, changing the order or the wording, or highlighting an especially important part. Collectively, even small changes will prove very worthwhile.

There is no reason to stop at one checklist. As time goes on, you may develop a whole series of them for different situations. For example, I have different checklists for reviewing non-financial shares and a separate one for financials; I also have checklists to complete before putting on any buy or sell order. The key is to always specify clearly at the top when each checklist is to be used.

In addition, checklists are likely to be more effective if you can get the format right. This is not just a presentational issue. A checklist that is too vague or too long is unlikely to get followed thoroughly. Some helpful tips are:

1. Keep it brief: five to ten items is normally enough. It should certainly fit comfortably on one page.

2. Use simple and precise wording that cannot be misconstrued.

3. Use a large, easy-to-read font.

Something else I find extremely helpful is to use colours. Colours can be used to separate different sections or to highlight especially important checks. A very useful trick is to combine a checklist with a traffic-light system. So when a company scores well on a factor I give it a green check, if it is okay it gets an orange check and if it scores badly it gets a red check. This makes it very easy to see at a glance where the strengths and weaknesses lie and what requires further investigation or monitoring.

A final idea to consider is building pause points into your checklists. A pause point is where you stop and look over the work you have just done as well as preparing for the next steps. They are a useful way to check you're doing things correctly, and not just ticking mindlessly, taking shortcuts or skipping steps.

For example, I always self-impose a one-hour cooling-off period before placing any deal. This is used to revisit the main assumptions, and to double-check the main checklist points as well as the dealing paperwork. It is surprising how often I stop myself or make a different decision as a result of these pause points.

An example of an Investment Checklist is shown below.

Learning to love your checklists

In spite of the success of checklists, they are used by only a tiny minority of people outside of the airline industry. Even with the incredible returns achieved by the checklist-users in the venture capital industry, they have been and remain a tiny minority.

The fact is that checklists are incredibly unpopular: people do not like using them. People prefer to rely on their own natural instincts and flair. Moreover, it seems that highly intelligent people in skilled sectors are the most reluctant to use checklists, even though they stand to benefit the most. As Gawande observes:

> "We don't like checklists. They can be painstaking. They're not much fun. But I don't think the issue here is mere laziness. There's something deeper, more visceral going on when people walk away not only from saving lives but from making money. It somehow feels beneath us to use a checklist, an embarrassment. It runs counter to deeply held beliefs about how the truly great handle situations of high stakes and complexity. The truly great are daring. They improvise. They do not have protocols and checklists."[85]

The point is that to benefit from checklists you have to be able to get over your ego. You have to be willing to accept your flaws and appreciate that personal brilliance or good fortune might not be

---

85. *Ibid.*, p. 173

Global Value Checklist

(Read and complete checklist during initial stock appraisal)

Preliminaries		
	Print off this sheet - Follow the checklist!!!	
Stock		
Source		
Date		
Size & liquidity	>$200m Market Cap, Average daily value traded > $1m	
Phase		
Underperformance: Is it at a depressed point in its cycle?	Weak share price over 3-5 years	
	5yr Sales growth = weak/moderate	
	20 year RoE and margin record: Overearning? What is normal?	
	Asset growth (avoid booming capex or assets)	
	Check Asset turnover (avoid low/falling)	
Ownership

Need at least 2 for green light | Large Inside ownership / activist or concentrated owners | |
	Multi Insider (officers, directors, large holders) buys over past 6 months?	
	Buybacks or self-tenders (Δ shares o/s long term and short term)	
	Decent divi - Consistent? / Growing? / Initiated? / > 5%?	
	Long-term RoE record (high/low? Rising/falling? Stable/volatile?)	
Financial strength

IF WEAK => STOP! Esp. Walk away if not consistent record of making money!! | Net debt / EBITDA and Net debt/Equity (ideally should be low and falling) | |
	If Debt - check profile and currency match	
	Current ratio	
	Check fixed charge cover = EBITR / (Interest exp + R) => ! avoid if < 2 !	
	Check L-term Op Cash Flow, Free Cash Flow & Op. profitability record	
	***Check recent Quarters and forecasts for CFO, FCF & Op profitability ***	
Funding & capital discipline	Beware cash guzzlers => need long-term record of negative Cash from Financing	
	Check short-term record and outlook for -ve Cash From Financing	
	Need good 3 year discipline: LOW capex, M&A, dilution; HIGH buybacks, divis, debt paydown	
	Check for growth in debt / equity issuance / convertibles	

Historic / Relative Valuation	Sensecheck => EV/Sales: Low in absolute? Low versus history?	
	Sensecheck => Long term (7-yr average) P/E (Ideally less than 5, certainly < 10x)	
	Sensecheck => P/Book: Low in absolute? Low versus history ?	
	Sensecheck => Is it cheap versus relevant peer group multiples	

Pause point: stop here if not perfect

Earnings Quality / Accruals	Check 3 yr FCF and CFO > Net income	
	Check recent Quarters FCF and CFO > Net income	
	Check Working Capital: Inventory Days, Days Receivable, Cash Conv Cycle not blowing out	
Due Diligence	Beware of large / diversifying acquisitions - esp. Where core business is troubled	
	!! Read Financial Statements	
	Check auditor's letter and comments (may contain subtle messages??)	
	Check commitments and contingencies (esp. Off-Balance Sheet)	
	Check management remuneration	
	Check related party transactions	
	Check for capitalised expenses etc (esp. relevant for normalised profitability)	
Company Filings	Go through company filings and company website	
What am I missing?	Google around, check recent news, broker notes, investor blogs, contacts & experts	
Valuation	Make sure to include minorities & prefs and that minorities are fairly valued	
	Make sure to include unfunded pensions, provisions, commitments, contingent liabs etc	
	Check Accounts Currency vs. Exchange Currency	
	Use fully diluted shares (incl. convertibles, options, warrants etc)	
	Bear in mind the value of high Research or Marketing expenditure creating future value	

enough. Checklists *demand humility*. In most cases where checklists have been applied successfully, it began with a failure. Boeing introduced their airline checklists after the tragic crash of the Model 299. It took a fatal crash and the near-bankruptcy of the company to push them towards such a solution.

If you can get over your ego and embrace checklists, they will not only make you perform better, but, counter-intuitively, they actually allow brilliance to shine through even more. As Gawande explains:

> "The fear people have is rigidity. They imagine mindless automatons, heads down in a checklist, incapable of looking up and coping with the real world in front of them. But what you find, when a checklist is well made, is exactly the opposite. The checklist gets the dumb stuff out of the way, the routines your brain shouldn't have to occupy itself with... and lets it rise above to focus on the hard stuff."[86]

In summary, checklists are the perfect tool for value investors. Value investing is simple and highly profitable, yet very difficult to apply in practice. Checklists make the task so much easier. It is extraordinary that something so simple, quick and costless can prove so effective. A clear set of checklists is the best tool a value investor can have.

9.5 To finish first you must first finish

There is no shortage of so-called experts giving out investment advice. But the ones who deserve the most attention tend to be the oldest. The investment careers of legends such as Irving Khan, Walter Schloss, John Templeton, Charlie Munger and Warren Buffett all span well over half a century.

What makes these investors so remarkable and so rare is that they have managed to invest successfully for so long without blowing up. Failure rates in the investment world are terrifying. Of the 335 equity mutual

---

86. *Ibid.*, p. 177.

funds around in 1970, only 132 survived the next 25 years, and of those only 24 had outperformed after fees. In the hedge fund world, failure rates are estimated at 10% to 20% per annum. For every well-publicised success there are literally thousands of failures.

Over the very long term the vast majority of investors either do poorly or do not survive. In the short term however, many investors can appear to be incredibly successful. Sometimes this is down to blind luck. More commonly short-term success is achieved by taking on too much risk. Investors taking excessive risk will often put in stunning performances for several quarters or even years, only to get wiped out later on.

In the long run those sorts of risks are not worth taking. You'd be better off just leaving your money in a bank account than making 30% returns for nine years and losing 90% or 100% in year ten. An analogy is often drawn between financial risk and driving. You're better off driving at 50 and always getting where you want to go than driving at 80 and crashing.

To survive the enormous ups and downs that long-term investors face, any investment strategy must be highly resilient. Strategies that blow up do so because they underestimate how extreme market moves can be. There have been countless instances of sophisticated hedge funds losing all their money and the perplexed whizz-kid in charge saying, "I can't believe it, this is a one-in-a-billion-year event."

The danger with relying on conventional models is that markets often go to even bigger extremes than are predicted by those models. This is partly down to the human behavioural biases mentioned earlier and it also has a lot to do with feedback loops. Feedback loops are where one positive or negative event has knock-on effects, like a line of dominoes. Good or bad events feed off each other, spiralling further and further out of control.

The global financial crisis was an example. Modelling problems in US sub-prime mortgages would not have predicted the crisis, because what mattered were the knock-on effects. Since feedback loops like this are actually quite common, the investor needs to be resilient enough to withstand them, and ideally to profit from them.

Building resilience

There are some simple things investors can do to ensure their strategy is sufficiently resilient. I would say all of these are necessities for the long-term value investor.

Avoid leverage and be willing to hold a little cash

If you borrow to invest (through debt, margin or derivatives), it will interfere with your survivability. As Jeremy Grantham explains, "Leverage reduces the investor's critical asset: Patience." If you buy deeply undervalued shares you will make handsome long-run returns, *providing you can wait*. Value investors do not need leverage. In addition, if you are struggling to find attractive new investments, be willing to hold at least a few percent in cash. This will allow you to act flexibly and opportunistically.

Don't get into a position where you might face a liquidity squeeze

This is especially the case for professional fund managers, but it can also hit individual investors who may need to sell a lot when markets are weak. Liquidity squeezes occur when an investor is forced to sell a large volume of shares at short notice. This can often knock the price severely, especially in a bear market. Avoid taking large positions in illiquid shares or planning for higher liquidity than can comfortably be achieved.

Avoid too much weakness in the underlying holdings

We have already seen how important financial strength is for value investors. Sometimes weak value shares will have a strong run in a bull market and then collapse violently when sentiment or the economy turns. It is highly dangerous to have too many of these. Something I find helpful is to have a *danger bucket*. This is the section of my portfolio that contains shares where it is foreseeable they might require external financing. I aim to keep this to below 15% of the total portfolio.

Diversify

We've already seen that there are many different iterations of value investing and that not everything works all the time. Risks can be moderated and returns improved by running a diversified portfolio. This is not just about the number of holdings, but also how well spread they are in terms of size, geography and style. This is where it really helps to have flexible approaches to value investing.

Resist or avoid short-term benchmarks and targets

When strategist Dylan Grice launched his fund, he told prospective clients, "We don't have any targets. We have a process."[87] Because shares and whole markets can veer wildly from fair value for a long time, and because luck can have an enormous influence over the short term, short-term targets make no sense. They can also be incredibly damaging, pushing investors to act foolishly in order to meet them. The process is the bit you can control – trying to meet short-term targets will just get in the way.

Contrarian value investing is the ultimate risk management tool

One of the great things about contrarian value investing is that many of its features actually counter excessive risk anyway.

First of all, if you're buying cheap and out-of-favour businesses you're unlikely to get caught up in a bubble. In fact, you're much more likely to be buying at the bottom of a feedback loop than the top. If you look at many of the biggest financial blow-ups, they occurred because investors bought more as prices went up. Again, US housing provides a classic example. As buyers made more money they added more leverage and bought more and more expensive houses. Investors in the tech bubble did exactly the same. This is exactly the opposite of what a contrarian does.

---

87. Grice, D., 'Popular Delusions. The Tyranny of Targets: Process, Outcome and the Complexity of it All', Société Générale Cross Asset Research, Global Strategy (June 2012).

Moreover, contrarian investments are themselves less risky. Bad things happen when the outlook is good and the price is high, then something unexpected goes wrong. When the problems are known and everyone is fearful, risk is actually lower because those problems can be seen and people are out trying to resolve them. This is what Howard Marks calls "the perversity of risk."

And the final, crucial point is that value investors do not buy overvalued assets. Risk is not determined by asset quality: the price of an asset is the principal determinant of its riskiness. Overpriced assets are dangerous regardless of their quality. A portfolio of undervalued assets that can be held patiently is a far less risky proposition.

Add all this together and it becomes clear why contrarian value works not just in terms of pure investment returns, but risk management too.

9.6 Summary

- The vast majority of value investors fail to consistently follow a sound strategy. Consequently they achieve disappointing long-term results.

- Value investing is quite simple in theory but difficult in practice, due to psychological factors, distractions, information overload and, in the case of professional investors, institutional pressures.

- Value investing works better when undertaken by one or two independently-minded individuals, rather than committees or hierarchies.

- To invest successfully you need a clear plan that you can follow consistently.

- A plan is much easier to stick to if:

  - You make it yours. Take the time and effort to come up with something you really understand and believe in.

- You keep it simple: far simpler than you think you can cope with.

- You have realistic expectations about results, volatility and the unevenness of returns.

- You focus on execution, not outcomes.

- Use checklists: they are the perfect tool for the value investor.

- Good checklists lead to consistency, cut out mistakes and help you to get the basics right, even under pressure.

- Checklists provide a pathway to improvement. They should evolve and develop over time.

- Remember: most investors fail to execute well. They let their ego get in the way of sticking to the simple rules that matter most.

- To achieve good long-term outcomes, make your strategy resilient:

  - Avoid leverage and be willing to hold a little cash occasionally.

  - Don't get into liquidity squeezes.

  - Avoid a large proportion of weakly financed holdings (danger bucket).

  - Diversify.

  - Avoid short-term targets.

- Applying a contrarian approach will protect you from the biggest investment risks.

CHAPTER 10.

The Way Ahead

10.1 Never stop improving

"The big difference between those who are successful and those who are not is that successful people learn from their mistakes and the mistakes of others."

Sir John Templeton[88]

Successful investors constantly evolve and improve. As time goes on, all this progress adds up to quite a lot. This book is just the beginning of that journey. The hard part is continuing the journey.

Active investing means experimenting and inevitably making mistakes. There is no way to avoid this. As Joel Greenblatt commented, "Some

---

88. Templeton, J. M., '16 Rules for Investment Success', reprinted by Franklin Templeton Investments (1993).

things you have to learn by doing them wrong, so I encourage people to risk being wrong. You can't be a good investor without investing."[89]

Do not be afraid to experiment and to try new techniques. This is especially important early on in a career. It takes a long time to improve and the ability to start early will be an invaluable advantage. If you can find ways to experiment where there is little serious impact if you do get things wrong, so much the better. Being in such a position will give you the courage to experiment freely.

What separates those who succeed from those who do not, is that the successful identify their mistakes and weaknesses, acknowledge them, and learn from them by making deliberate improvements. While most investors prefer to brush over past misjudgments, successful investors regard them as valuable treasures. Each one is worth examining and considering. Each one may contain the potential to become better.

This is the basis of progress. The burgeoning field of performance science identifies people's most common and basic mistakes and then comes up with ways to avoid them. From footballers to musicians, the improvements in performance are stunning. Meanwhile, car and aeroplane manufacturers have made incredible gains in performance, safety and reliability simply by experimenting constantly and looking for the slightest problem (an average mass-market car today will have done over a million miles in test drives). The right attitude is to want to find problems.

To be successful at investing, you must be willing to adopt the same attitude. You have to be honest with yourself. Keep a precise record of your decision-making and acknowledge where you get things wrong. In addition, actively seek out other investors you respect for criticism and feedback. The surest way to make more money is to make fewer mistakes.

---

89. Greenblatt, J., Interview in 'Graham & Doddsville; An investment newsletter from the students of Columbia Business School' (Issue 16, Fall 2012).

10.2 The triumph of the optimist

Throughout history there have always been doomsayers, predict imminent catastrophe for humanity. Yet, again and again, people triumphed against the odds. In the recent financial chaos, pessimism became exceptionally fashionable, especially for the media, who understand all too well the popular hunger for apocalyptic predictions.

And yet, as always, there is much to be optimistic about. Progress continues; good people and good businesses mostly get rewarded, and vice versa. As ever, people like to do good, and enjoy making others happy and contributing to progress.

In his landmark television series, *Civilisation*, Kenneth Clark, surveying 2000 years of Western History, observed that the greatest threat to civilisation and progress is not optimism or even over-optimism, but *fear*. When people are fearful, they do not take risks, and that means they do not try new things – an absolute must for progress. Instead of building a future, they feed off the present. Everything, even the architecture, becomes temporary, built to get through today rather than with an eye on tomorrow. As Clark put it:

> "It is a lack of confidence, more than anything else, that kills a civilisation. We can destroy ourselves by cynicism and disillusion, just as effectively as by bombs."[90]

Progress is always a case of two steps forward and one step back. Most of the time you want to be optimistic about the world. Only rarely does over-optimism extend to the point of decadence, when it justifies standing out from the crowd and taking a more timid stance.

So enjoy your investing. Not so much for the money but for the pleasure of the journey. Be happy, search out progress and seek to inspire it; otherwise what purpose does investing hold?

History has shown again and again the worth of optimism, and of value investing. Looking to the future, rarely, if ever, has there been so much for value investors to be optimistic about.

---

90. *Civilisation, Episode 13, Heroic Materialism*, TV Series, BBC (1969).

:ally matters.

ons should be based on an independent ·ssment of intrinsic worth.

f safety is always essential.

ı (versus history, peers and the market) as a sense-check.

- Look for bargains among the cheapest shares.

- Be flexible.

  - There is a season to everything, so have a range of valuation techniques and search strategies, including a willingness to look at high-quality shares.

  - Search and invest globally, especially among really cheap or out-of-favour markets.

  - Be able to invest in small or illiquid shares as much as is practicable.

- Focus on financial strength.

  - Buying undervalued shares with strong financials is the best way to avoid value traps.

  - Financial strength requires both strong liquidity (especially cash flows) and solvency.

  - Look across a broad range of measures and look for trends as well.

  - When assessing intrinsic value, be sure to include all the major non-operating assets and liabilities.

  - Take the time to read the financial statements and accompanying notes.

  - Incorporate financial strength in search strategies or screens, alongside valuation.

- Look for capital discipline.

- Invest in companies that are either permanently disciplined or deep into the retrenchment phase of their capital cycle.
- The historic records and current levels of shareholder yield and cash from financing are especially valuable indicators.

- Look for responsible stewardship.
  - How the company is managed is a vital determinant of its true worth. Look for well aligned owners and a management record of shareholder-friendly actions. Be very wary of the opposite.
  - Avoid companies with a lot of red flags or very serious red flags.

- Be contrarian.
  - To be very successful at investing means being very different from those around you. To do so requires facing up to enormous psychological and institutional barriers. This is really hard.
  - Value investing goes hand in hand with contrarian investing. The most significant undervaluations tend to be among the most unfavoured shares.
  - Look among the long-term dogs and the most hated or neglected shares.
  - Invest into deep crises.

- Be patient.
  - It can take a long time to find a really great investment. Be willing to wait and keep searching.
  - Value shares typically take several years to work out. Don't give up on them by expecting too much too soon.

- Value investing is nothing without consistent execution.
  - Value investing is simple and incredibly effective. The reason it keeps working is that it is incredibly hard to do.
  - Before you start, devise a clear and simple plan, with realistic expectations.
  - Focus on the process and how well you are executing, not on the outcomes. Never focus on near-term performance numbers.

- Use checklists to ensure consistent execution and to make deliberate improvements.
- Use a spreadsheet with buy and sell gates to ensure a consistent approach to buying, selling and rebalancing.
- Never stop improving.
  - Mistakes can be invaluable. Set aside time to candidly go over your mistakes and to learn from them.
  - Have ways to implement improvements deliberately.
  - Look for challenge and ideas from others whom you respect or who think differently.

Enjoy the journey!

INDEX

Lightning Source UK Ltd.
Milton Keynes UK
UKOW01f2343250917
309875UK00007B/323/P